When Wallflowers Dance
Becoming a Woman
of Righteous Confidence

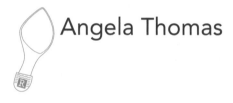 Angela Thomas

Leader and Retreat Guides by Jessica Weaver

LifeWay Press®
Nashville, Tennessee

Published by LifeWay Press®
© 2008 Angela Thomas

ISBN 978-1-4158-5432-3
Item 005139422

This book is the resource for CG-1333 in the subject areas
Personal Life and Women's Enrichment in the Christian Growth Study Plan.

Dewey Decimal classification: 248.843
Subject heading: WOMEN \ SELF-CONFIDENCE

Unless otherwise noted, all Scripture quotations are taken from the Holy Bible, New International Version, copyright © 1973, 1978, 1984 by International Bible Society.

Scripture quotations marked MSG are from *The Message* by Eugene Peterson. Copyright © 1993, 1994, 1995, 1996, 2000, 2001, 2002. Used by permission of NavPress Publishing Group.

Scripture quotations marked NASB are from the New American Standard Bible, copyright © 1960, 1962, 1963, 1971, 1972, 1973, 1975, 1977, 1995 by the Lockman Foundation. Used by permission. (*www.lockman.org*)

Scripture quotations marked NCV are from the New Century Version®. Copyright © 1987, 1988, 1991 by Thomas Nelson, Inc. Used by permission. All rights reserved.

Scripture quotations marked NLT are taken from the Holy Bible, New Living Translation, copyright © 1996, 2004. Used by permission of Tyndale House Publishers, Inc., Wheaton, IL 60189 USA. All rights reserved.

To order additional copies of this resource, write to LifeWay Church Resources Customer Service; One LifeWay Plaza; Nashville, TN 37234-0013; fax (615) 251-5933; call toll-free (800) 458-2772; order online at *www.lifeway.com*; e-mail *orderentry@lifeway.com*; or visit the LifeWay Christian store serving you.

Printed in the United States of America

Leadership and Adult Publishing
LifeWay Church Resources
One LifeWay Plaza
Nashville, TN 37234-0175

Contents

About the Author

Angela Thomas is a mother, best-selling author, speaker, and teacher. She is a woman in desperate pursuit of God. Her determination to know God on an intimate level and her dedication to studying the Bible have taught her many truths, some discovered through tears and some in times of joy.

Angela graduated from the University of North Carolina at Chapel Hill with a double major in economics and television production. She began full-time work in the field of transportation, but it was her avocation as part-time youth director that led her to enroll at Dallas Theological Seminary. She earned her Masters degree in Dallas and moved to North Carolina to become a minister to senior-high girls. Marriage and babies followed not long after, providing Angela with much joy … and much change.

Angela wrote her fist book, *Prayers for Expectant Mothers,* during her fourth pregnancy and followed it with *Prayers for New Mothers.* Her 2001 Focus on the Family release, *Tender Mercy for a Mother's Soul,* became a best seller.

Angela's writing had grown naturally out of her day-to-day life as a mother and as a woman. "I promised God I would tell the truth about my life and His work within me. My writing is just an extension of that. I'm really a storyteller, sharing out of my own life experiences."

Angela's other best-selling writings include *Do You Think I'm Beautiful?, A Beautiful Offering, Beautiful* (for young women), *Wild About You* (for students), and *My Single Mom Life.*

Angela speaks at conferences, retreats, and Bible studies across the country. Audiences enthusiastically respond to her practical, relevant discussions, and she instantly bonds with all types of women. Without the wrappings of pretense or pride, Angela tells it like it is … and how it can be.

Angela and her children, AnnaGrace, William, Grayson, and Taylor, reside in Knoxville, Tennessee. Angela, a single mom, is heavily involved at Two Rivers Church, where her family has attended since moving to Knoxville.

Jessica Weaver wrote the leader and retreat materials for this study. A graduate of the University of Richmond, Jessie is now an editor at LifeWay Christian Resources in Nashville, where she lives with her husband, Adam, and their cocker spaniel, Chester.

Introduction

My dear friend,

Most of my life I have felt like some sort of wallflower. In my awkward high-school years, I was the textbook wallflower in glasses and braces. Smart and active, but unknown. No votes for Homecoming court. No dates. And no one to ask me to dance.

As time went by, the physical attributes of wallflower began to fade, but its spirit was never far away. In every little defeat or big discouragement, I'd retreat into the heartache of being unseen and unknown. Eventually, it seemed as if I were destined to play the wallflower role forever. As it turns out, the woman who retreats into the spirit of wallflower eventually becomes an un-woman. Empty. Numb. Barely present. Just breathing, smiling, and blending in to stay out of the way.

As long as I can remember, I have known of God and believed in His existence; but one day, in the middle of my wallflower years, that truth became mine. I called God my Father and claimed Jesus as my Savior. As purely as I knew how, I wanted to return God's love with my life. But mine was a wallflower life, and I assumed it would continue to be that way with God.

Our God is a pursuing God. God dragged me out of the dark and into the light. He held me close and gave me safety. As I came to know deeper truths of His desire and passion for me, the most beautiful picture I could paint of His love was the picture of a wallflower being asked to dance.

This study is about dancing—about not just living with God but spiritually maturing to dance in His arms. About responding, "Yes," when He chooses you and asks, "Would you like to?" I believe that answer requires total surrender to God's sovereign will and a complete trust in His tender love. The woman who is dancing with God is captivating.

Here is the good news of the gospel: God is coming across heaven and earth for you. Maybe you have already met Him. Maybe you are just beginning to hear His voice and recognize His glorious presence in your ordinary life. Either way, He is already here, pursuing your heart. Inviting you to step away from the edge of your life and into the center of His passion.

My dear friend, lift up your weary head. Look into the eyes of your Heavenly Father. When God is in the room, all of the wallflowers get to dance.

Looking out from His arms,
Angela

Sometimes it's just one foot in front of the other. Throw your feet over the side of the bed. Strap on the shoes that make you feel pretty. And decide to move in the direction of the woman you've always wanted to become.

Come to the Altar

Week 1

Come to the Altar

Hello, my friend. I am sitting in the comfy chair in my study. The kids are at school, and I just made a fresh pot of coffee. My laptop is perched on my knees, my Bible is propped up beside me, and I have been praying for us. I am so very excited about the next six weeks and this growth journey we will take together.

Beginning this study is like we have come to the altar together. Today we bend our hearts over the awesomeness of God. We humble ourselves in His majestic presence. We bow our heads in reverence and take deep breaths of His glory.

Before we begin, it seems the right thing for us to do is actually find an altar or a place around you right now that can become an altar. I have an ottoman in front of me, and so this morning that piece of furniture will become an altar. Maybe you see the corner of your bed or the chair in your kitchen or office. Maybe it's the hearth of a fireplace or the simple act of laying a bath towel across the floor. So to begin, look around and find a place where you can kneel or bend or even lie on your face.

Now, come to the altar. Literally. Prayerfully. Come. As you come, remember whom you kneel before. Pray this psalm back to the Lord as you remember and rejoice in the character of our God:

> O Lord, our Lord,
> > how majestic is your name in all the earth!
>
> You have set your glory
> > above the heavens.
> From the lips of children and infants
> > you have ordained praise
> because of your enemies,
> > to silence the foe and the avenger.
>
> When I consider your heavens,
> > the work of your fingers,
> the moon and the stars,
> > which you have set in place,
> what is man that you are mindful of him,
> > the son of man that you care for him?

You made him a little lower than the heavenly beings
and crowned him with glory and honor.

You made him ruler over the works of your hands;
you put everything under his feet:
all flocks and herds,
and the beasts of the field,
the birds of the air,
and the fish of the sea,
all that swim the paths of the seas.

O LORD, our Lord,
how majestic is your name in all the earth!
Psalm 8

We've begun today's study by praying an entire chapter of the Bible. Every day of this study, I will ask you to pray a verse of Scripture back to God as an offering of praise. What if praise becomes a habit? What if first thing, before anything else, we come to God with a grateful heart? It might just keep our hearts exactly where they are supposed to be. And our minds will filter everything that comes next through the context of thankfulness.

Let's continue with the praise you are bringing to the altar. Now remember who God is to you personally. How He cares for you. The gifts He has given.

Use the space below to thank Him with a prayer written from your heart.

How have you come to the altar today? Circle all of the following words that apply to where you are right now.

weary	anxious	excited
burdened	hopeful	numb
hurting	empty	discouraged
hopeless	searching	blessed
happy	lost	overwhelmed
hesitant	eager	worried
content	afraid	spiritually thirsty
rejected	disappointed	full of love
sick	confused	

Maybe you have something so heavy on your heart that you need to write the details here (in words or in code) to bring the burden from the dark into the light.

Now, everything you have written or circled ... the truth of where you are right now ... this is the time to lay it on the altar. Maybe you will speak these truths to God in prayer. Maybe you will lay your hands over this page and pray out loud over each one. However God leads you to respond, bring who you are, what you carry, and all that you hold in your heart to the altar of your loving God.

These next six weeks are about growing up in the faith. About you and me learning together about becoming mature followers of Christ. Passionate. Alive. Amazing. Forgiven. Rejoicing women. Many of us have lived wallflower lives with God. Standing back. Watching. Hesitant. Wanting more but afraid to try. Seeing others but believing it could never be us.

In this study I am praying for a spiritual growth that will shape and re-shape your heart for God. Are you ready to grow again, or maybe grow for the very first time?

Mark the sentence that corresponds to where you are:

☐ Ready to get going ... yippee. Woohoo. I love this stuff!!
☐ My head says I need to, but I'm just so tired.
☐ I've never done anything like this before. Ready but hesitant.
☐ My friend made me join this study.

You already know that the years are going by too fast. We have only so many days appointed to us. Only so much time to live amazing, redeemed lives. What if your procrastination ends today? What if we decide together to do whatever God determines to grow us up in our faith? Maybe you are excited or maybe you are present but numb. Either way, God is still God, and His Word to you in these weeks is going to be powerful!

We will never become godly women just standing around waiting for godliness to descend on a cloud. We won't wake up

We will never become godly women just standing around waiting for godliness to descend on a cloud.

one morning and be amazing. We will only become the women God had in mind because we have decided. Decided to pursue God and the truth of His Word. Decided to lay aside the distraction and run toward the glory. Decided to lay our hearts on His altar and stay there, safe in His arms. Understanding the deeper truths of God's love for me has been like being the wallflower who was asked to dance.

So dance we shall, my friend. May your heart leap with anticipation. We have begun on the altar of our majestic Lord. There is no sweeter way to begin with God than the cleansing act of surrender. See you tomorrow.

Day 2

Growing Up

Hello my friend. I am praying today that you remember how it felt to lay your life and your right-now truth on the altar of God yesterday. I am also praying that the sweetness of that surrender will keep giving you a big, deep spiritual breath.

Has there ever been a time you felt as if you'd been given a "big, deep spiritual breath"? If so, describe the situation.

Just a word about surrender and laying our lives on the altar of God. It is truly a choice we must make every day. The woman who is growing spiritually will come each morning and bend her heart over the reverent truth of who God is. He is God, and we are not. He is holy, and we keep falling short. He is Savior, and we desperately need Him every day.

So today, take just a moment to remember the altar where you laid your heart and the beautiful, amazing God who waits for you there.

In this study, I will usually include the verses of Scripture that we discuss each day. But just because the verse may be printed on this page, it doesn't mean that you shouldn't also look at the passage in your own Bible. Opening your own Bible is a big part of learning your way around the Scripture. The Bible becomes less intimidating when you begin to feel comfortable with how it's organized and where things are in your own personal copy.

I love having my own Bible everywhere I go: traveling, at home, or out for a quiet afternoon. It's the one thing I always take with me. A couple of times, I have left my Bible in my room while I was traveling and used someone else's to teach. I felt off-kilter the whole time. Having your own copy of God's Word is important. If you don't have a Bible you love or a translation that's easy for you to understand, then make that purchase a top priority. Better yet, choose the one you like and put it on your birthday wish list. What a perfect gift for a woman who is becoming passionate about her relationship with Jesus!

So with all that said, turn in your Bible to 1 Peter 2:2-3:

Like newborn babies, crave pure spiritual milk, so that by it you may grow up in your salvation, now that you have tasted that the Lord is good.

What things do you currently "crave"?

What do you think "spiritual milk" means?

When I read these verses, it's really hard not to take this passage personally. No matter how many times I read these words, I know that God is speaking directly to me. So how about we make this verse personal together? Fill in the following blanks with me:

_____ (your name), be

like a _____ baby. Crave pure

_____ milk. So that with the craving, you will

_____ _____ in your salvation. Do this because you

have _____ that the Lord is good.

A Girlfriend Nudge

I'll give you a gentle push every so often in this study. Just a little "grow in your knowledge" nudge so that you can learn more if you want more. So today, your nudge is about the books of the Bible. Do you know the books of the New Testament in order? Not kinda, sorta. Really. It will give you so much confidence to be able to find a reference in no time flat. So here's the nudge.

Memorize the New Testament books in order.

THEN say them out loud to a friend or your spouse or show off to the kids after you call out their spelling words.

Over and over, this verse has been so powerful to me. Every time I read it, I hear God calling me toward more and more spiritual maturity. Every time, I hear Him remind me to desire pure spiritual nourishment—and with that food to keep growing up in the truth of my salvation.

Now here's the foundation of the verse ... you and I should crave spiritual growth because we have tasted that the Lord is good! Have you tasted the goodness of God?

Quickly, give me the top three ways you have tasted in the goodness of the Lord this past year:

1.

2.

3.

We have all tasted the goodness of God. But how we sometimes forget. This passage teaches that when we have tasted, the natural result is growth. You and I will grow up in our salvation. Do you hear the personal and tender instruction? If you have tasted that the Lord is good, then grow, sister! Don't be satisfied with who you are or who you have been. Don't procrastinate. Don't turn away or shut down to this great truth ... grow, baby!

We are going to pick back up here tomorrow, but before we wrap it up, I want you to think about what may have kept you from growing your faith in the past. For me some seasons of life have seemed to bring explosive and sustained spiritual growth. Then I've had those years when my growth was scattered and small. I have loved God all this time, but life gives us many challenges to face.

My years with little babies at home were sometimes more like spiritual survival than growth. The months surrounding my divorce were barely about survival. I can look back and see the lessons I learned when I just held onto God, but my desire is to consciously be growing in spiritual truth and maturity, even through the trials and difficult years.

So how about you? What hinders or keeps you from going to the next step of growth with God? Distraction? Forgetfulness? Difficult circumstances?

I am praying that this six weeks will become a spiritual mile marker for us. No matter what has kept us from growing in the past, I believe God will use these weeks to conquer our inadequacies and take us to the next patch of holy ground.

Let's believe God together for a season of spiritual growth unlike anything we have ever known!

Day 3

Salvation

Let's pretend you've received an inheritance.

An attorney calls you and says all the members of your family will receive a gift. You will each receive equal shares by virtue of belonging to the family. He asks you to come to his office next Tuesday around noon to receive your inheritance.

So Tuesday comes, and you keep your appointment. The attorney gingerly shakes your hand and then tells you that your wealth is vast. There are many facets to your birthright. Many ways in which much has been given to you. He gives you a beautiful leather-bound chest and explains that all the dimensions of your wealth will be found inside.

You gratefully take the exquisite chest home. Then you decide it would look perfect on the bedside table in your room. Occasionally you peek inside the chest, but you never really explore all that has been given through your inheritance. You feel really happy to be in the family, but the inheritance goes unexplored. All the wealth that rightfully belongs to you never has any influence in your life, nor do you ever enjoy the proceeds that could have come from its investment.

Daily Prayer Praise

To the only God our Savior be glory, majesty, power and authority, through Jesus Christ our Lord, before all ages, now and forevermore! Amen.

Jude 25

But you have the treasure. It will always be yours. No one can ever take it away. It's just that so much more waited for you ... if you had only opened the gift and explored it.

I know it's just a silly story, but the truth is that when you ask Jesus to be your Savior, you have received the great treasure of your salvation. Today I want us to begin talking about the wealth you receive through salvation. But first ...

When did you ask Jesus to be your Savior?

What is the story of your salvation?

I want you to know something ... if the last two questions left you with doubt, you are not alone. Many women have known about Jesus, or heard of Him, maybe even studied His teachings, but they doubt that real salvation has ever come to them.

I remember as a high school and college student never being sure I'd gotten it right. I must have asked Jesus to be my Savior at least 175 times. No kidding. Finally, one day in prayer, I was mulling over my doubts when I was sure I heard God say, "Angela, I heard you the first time."

Maybe you have doubts, even the slightest doubt. Or maybe you just never got around to asking Jesus to be your Savior. This is the best time to settle those doubts forever.

Here are the most powerful truths you will ever hear:

Our God, your Creator, is loving and holy.

He created you to live in a love relationship with Him. He planned for you to bring Him glory with your life.

But all of humanity became separated from God through sin. Me, you, all of us.

God's penalty for sin is death. Nothing can change the penalty. Payment is required from everyone who has sinned.

But God is love and His heart longs for you and me and all of creation to be restored through love.

And so, from the depths of God's enduring love, He sent His only son, Jesus, to pay the penalty of your sin and mine.

God declared that believing in His Son was the only way to be saved from the penalty of our sin.

So every woman, man, and child who responds to God's call and places their faith in Jesus—who tells God, "I believe that Your Son, Jesus, paid for my sin," is thereby saved from penalty. And the person who believes is given the treasure we call salvation.

Every saved person becomes a member of the family of God.

With your salvation comes an inheritance that could never be bought. A daughter of the King is rich indeed.

This one word "believe" represents all a sinner can do and all a sinner must do to be saved.
—Lewis Sperry Chafer [1]

I want us to spend the rest of this week talking about the riches given to us through salvation. Here is what I want you to understand: This wealth of our salvation is not just for someone else. God is talking to you, wherever you are and whatever circumstance you find yourself in.

Becoming a mature follower of Christ means that we open the treasure of our inheritance and explore the goodness and power that He has graciously given us. And then, maturity means that we not only *know* but we also *live* in the truths of God's love toward us.

This study is not about acquiring more knowledge, although studying the Bible always gives us more. Rather, I pray that we will begin to *live* these truths in new and powerful ways. That every aspect of who we are will be improved and made powerful because the truth of our salvation is becoming the truth of our everyday lives. I am praying for your relationships to be changed. Your mind to be renewed. Your heart to be encouraged. Your focus to be sharp.

This wealth of our salvation is not just for someone else. God is talking to you, wherever you are and whatever circumstance you find yourself in.

Think about your salvation. The God of heaven has rescued you from the penalty of eternal death. Not only has He given a gift for eternity, but God has also given you a wealth of spiritual gifts for this life on earth.

What if you spend a minute telling the Lord, "Thank You," followed by a commitment to unpack your inheritance? Maybe you can say something as simple as this:

Jesus, thank You for saving me from my sin. God, I want all the wealth You have given to me. All the inheritance of my salvation. Every good thing You have promised. I want to be a mature woman of God. Righteous, holy, a woman who lives what she has been given. In Jesus' name, amen.

Day 4

The Riches of Our Salvation

Daily Prayer Praise

I am the LORD, and there is no other; apart from me there is no God.

Isaiah 45:5

I hope it's beginning to sink in anew to you this week. God has given us such a blessing through the gift of our salvation. What a precious, gracious God we have.

God's altar is a place for all of us. There He embraces those who have known God for decades and those who consider themselves the lowest of sinners. You see, the altar of God's grace is for us all.

Maybe you look around the room during your Bible study and think to yourself, "What am I doing here?" I want to encourage you—no one has ever earned salvation. It is a gift to be received. That is the point. Such an undeserved gift should give you a grateful heart; and we are called to live grateful, spiritual lives because truly, we have tasted that the Lord is good.

Read the following verses with me:

But grow in the grace and knowledge of our Lord and Savior Jesus Christ. To him be glory both now and forever! Amen.
2 Peter 3:18

So if you're serious about living this new resurrection life with Christ, act like it. Pursue the things over which Christ presides. Don't

shuffle along, eyes to the ground, absorbed with the things right in front of you. Look up, and be alert to what is going on around Christ— that's where the action is. See things from his perspective.
Colossians 3:1-2, MSG

When you see the phrase "resurrection life," what words and phrases come to mind?

What do you think characterizes living a resurrection life?

Now write a little note of encouragement to yourself about pursuing God. Maybe you just begin with your name and write these verses back to yourself. What kind of spiritual motivation would speak to you right now?

A Girlfriend Nudge

Not one of us will ever wake up one morning to find that overnight we became a godly woman. You will have to decide that you want to become an amazing woman like that. Today, what if you say, "I have decided"?

If we're going to grow, I'd say we first have to open the treasure of our inheritance and begin looking at what we have been given. We'll go through these gifts from God like they are a list on the fridge, but don't let that devalue their importance. Linger over these truths. Take in each one deeply. My job is to help you grow and to encourage you to live each one more fully. Here we go!

The Treasures of our Inheritance

1. We have been reconciled by God.

Look at the following Scripture:

All this is from God, who reconciled us to himself through Christ and gave us the ministry of reconciliation: that God was reconciling

The Treasures of
Our Inheritance

1. We have been
reconciled by God.

the world to himself in Christ, not counting men's sins against them. And he has committed to us the message of reconciliation.
2 Corinthians 5:18-19

What reconciliation means for you and me is that at the moment of salvation,

We pass from God's wrath into God's blessing.

To be reconciled means that you move from conflict into a renewed relationship of compatibility and peace.

We go from the assurance of spiritual death into the assurance of spiritual life.

When you are reconciled by God, your sin is no longer counted against you.

Think about all of this for a minute. At the moment of salvation you inherit the blessing of God, and God's wrath toward you ends right in that moment. No more death. No more separation because of sin. Do you know what this means? God is not mad at you. You are in His family, and He wants to bless you. To give you a passionate spiritual life. To set you free from the guilt of sin. You belong to God now. You should bear the family likeness and enjoy the family blessings.

Have you ever believed God was mad at you?
☐ yes ☐ no

How did that feeling affect your personal relationship with Him?

Most of us are afraid to go near someone who's mad. Or if we do, we go reluctantly, waiting for their wrath or the lashing we fear is waiting. If you have believed that you still deserve God's wrath, you have not looked closely at the inheritance. Salvation means the debt has been canceled and the blessing is yours to keep. You are no longer an outsider looking in ... you are a member of the family of God.

2. We have been redeemed.

You have a coupon for a free loaf of bread. The coupon is basically a worthless piece of paper, but it has a promise attached. The promise is that if you come to a certain store with a little paper promise, a gift of bread waits for you. The store will exchange your coupon for a loaf of bread.

Jesus made a promise that goes something like this.

> Bring your life, all of it, the good, the bad and the worthless. I take broken-down lives on trade in. Believe in Me as your Savior and I will redeem your life with gifts you cannot contain. I will replace your despair with joy, your ashes for beauty, your heartache with hope.
> **(See Matt. 11:28; Luke 4:18-19.)**

The gift of salvation redeems your life. God removes the marks against you with a holy exchange for His glory.

Have you ever met someone who believed the past would always count against them? Have you ever felt that all your mistakes must surely add up somewhere to weigh the scales against you? To be redeemed means that God supernaturally makes you worthy of His love, even if you never thought that could happen for you.

The Bible says:

> He has rescued us from the dominion of darkness and brought us into the kingdom of the Son he loves, in whom we have redemption.
> **Colossians 1:13-14**

What about a big shout-out, thank-You, hallelujah prayer right about now?! Not only have we been rescued but salvation also takes the worthless and makes them righteous.

Good grief, we were just getting started with our treasures, and our time is already over. So let's pick up here tomorrow, but for the rest of today ... what if you remain grateful?

You have been given life instead of death!

Your old life has been exchanged for new plans and new purpose!

The Treasures of
Our Inheritance

1. We have been
   reconciled by God.
2. We have been
   redeemed.

Not only have we been rescued but salvation also takes the worthless and makes them righteous.

More Riches of Our Salvation

Daily Prayer Praise

O LORD God Almighty,
who is like you?
You are mighty,
O LORD, and your
faithfulness
surrounds you.

Psalm 89:8

The Treasures of
Our Inheritance

1. We have been
   reconciled by God.
2. We have been
   redeemed.
3. We are saved from
   condemnation.

If you are anything like me, everything else crowds into my mind and sometimes I just plain forget how rich I am because of Christ. I forget to remember; but when I set my mind to remember, God does this miraculous work in my soul. He restores my peace. He renews my hope. He gives the perspective I had lost in my overwhelmed life.

Today we will keep setting our minds on remembering. I pray that you don't just skim over these great theological truths. Good theology should lead to right living. And right living is the life God desires to bless. All that means that our families can be healed. Our heart can be renewed. There is great, great hope for our future.

More Treasure of Our Inheritance

3. We are saved from condemnation.

Maybe you've read the following verse a hundred times. I have even repeated it through the years in a song,

> *There is now no condemnation for those who are in Christ Jesus.*
> **Romans 8:1**

Now I want you to insert your name into this truth:

_____, you are no longer condemned. Not now on this earth, and not for all eternity. Jesus has saved you from condemnation.

And here is the kicker. When you have *received* no condemnation, you are supposed to *give* no condemnation. What if your kids received discipline without further condemnation? What if your spouse listened to your hurts but you did not follow with condemnation? Your coworkers? Your in-laws and out-laws?

What is the difference between loving discipline
and condemnation?

Do you believe it is possible to argue or give discipline without a
sense of condemnation?   ☐ yes ☐ no
Explain your answer here.

What new light on this issue does Hebrews 12:5-7 give you?

Did you ever expect harsh words that never came? Have you
sometimes thought you deserved consequences but none
followed? How does receiving no condemnation make you feel?

Jesus has saved us from continued condemnation. What does
that truth do in your soul?

How will go from this page today and give no condemnation, just
like Jesus has given to you?

*Have you forgotten
the encouraging words
God spoke to you as his
children? He said,
   "My child, don't
make light of the LORD's
discipline,
   and don't give up
when he corrects you.
   For the LORD
disciplines those he loves,
   and he punishes
each one he accepts as
his child."
   As you endure
this divine discipline,
remember that God is
treating you as his own
children. Who ever heard
of a child who is never
disciplined by its father?*
Hebrews 12:5-7, NLT

4. We have been made children of God.

You know how it is to be born into a family. That's it. You're in the family forever and ever, amen. To be saved means that we are forever born into the family of God. And we aren't just sneaking in, hoping they let us stay. God has made each one of us His very own child.

> *Beloved, now we are children of God.*
> **1 John 3:2, NASB**

> *I will be a Father to you, and you will be my sons and daughters, says the Lord Almighty.*
> **2 Corinthians 6:18**

Think about the children you know or the children you have. List five characteristics of a typical child's life. I'll get you started.

1. He is fed and clothed.

2. She is protected.

3.

4.

5.

6.

7.

A friend recently commented about this phenomenon—her daughter never sits up at night worrying about how Mom and Dad will take care of her, where the money will come from. She just rests in their protection. It's never crossed her mind that she won't be taken care of. Can you imagine feeling that same

The Treasures of
Our Inheritance

1. We have been
   reconciled by God.
2. We have been
   redeemed.
3. We are saved from
   condemnation.
4. We have been made
   children of God.

wonderful hedge of protection? It is exactly what we should expect to feel from God! Because of His promise never to leave us or forsake us, we can fully rest knowing He will protect us and provide for us.

Now reread your list, remembering that you have been made a child of God. Say it with me, "God is good."

5. We have been forgiven and justified.

Not only does the Lord promise to forgive all who believe in Jesus, He goes further and gives the gift of justification. Remember its definition this way:

Just-as-if-I'd-never-sinned.

God-forgiveness is deep and wide and sure and eternal. Then, because you are a child of God, He promises that you will be justified—treated as if you never sinned.

Look at these passages with me:

> *In him we have redemption through his blood, the forgiveness of sins, in accordance with the riches of God's grace.*
> **Ephesians 1:7**

> *Therefore, since we have been justified through faith, we have peace with God through our Lord Jesus Christ.*
> **Romans 5:1**

We are running out of time today, but I want us to see much more about the inheritance we have been given, so I'm going to load up the next treasure to overflowing and then leave you with a girlfriend nudge to go deeper.

6. We have been made objects.

Look at this listing; I think it will take your breath away.

We are the objects of God's love. —**Ephesians 2:4**

We are the objects of His grace. —**Ephesians 2:8**

We are the objects of His power. —**Ephesians 1:19**

We are the objects of His faithfulness. —**Hebrews 13:5**

The Treasures of
Our Inheritance

1. We have been reconciled by God.
2. We have been redeemed.
3. We are saved from condemnation.
4. We have been made children of God.
5. We have been forgiven and justified.
6. We have been made objects.

Believe it or not, we have only peeked i nside our inheritance these past two days. God has given us so much more. So if you want more, refill your coffee cup and jump in here:

We are delivered from darkness.
Colossians 1:13

We are chosen.
1 Peter 2:9

We are released from the law.
Romans 7:6

We have access to God.
Ephesians 2:18

We are heavenly citizens.
Philippians 3:20

We are light.
Ephesians 5:8

We are baptized, filled, and sealed with the Holy Spirit.
**1 Corinthians 12:13;
Romans 5:5;
Ephesians 4:30**

We have been given every spiritual blessing.
Ephesians 1

We are the objects of His peace. —**Colossians 3:15**

We are the objects of His consolation. —**2 Thessalonians 2:16-17**

We are the objects of His intercession. —**Hebrews 7:25**

Does this list do the same thing to you? These gifts of God come over me like a fresh wind clearing my mind. I just read back through each one, looked up every verse, and nothing about my day is the same. The thoughts that weighed like burdens a few moments ago have decreased in the light of these truths.

Look again at the list of objects. Which one do you need to remember most today?

Why?

I'd like for us to end this week just like we began: on the altar. Do you remember how you laid your life on the altar a few days ago? However you made an altar that day, return there for just a few minutes.

Think about what we've considered together this week. Salvation has been given to us. A gift attached with an unimaginable inheritance. Now it's time for you and for me to grow up to the next high place of our salvation.

Imagine what God could be dreaming for you … the woman who is growing up in her salvation. The wallflower who is learning to dance.

There is … a time to dance.
Ecclesiastes 3:1,4

---

1. Lewis Sperry Chafer, *Salvation: God's Marvelous Work of Grace* (Grand Rapids, MI: Kregel, 1991), 47.

Prayer

Father,

I love You. Really. Truly. I love You.

Thank You for this fresh start. A new study. A new book. A new journey. The next chapter of my faith in You.

I lay myself across your altar today and ask you to breathe into me a fresh desire for Your truth. A new thirst for righteousness. Would You return the joy of my salvation, times a million? Would You undo the tangles I have wound around my life? Would You be more real to me than I have ever experienced?

God, I want these weeks to change me, and I know change requires surrender. So my heart is on Your altar. Re-make the woman who bears this heart. Redirect every lost decision. Rekindle passion.

Come to me. Wash over me with Your presence. Surround me with Your holiness. I am here and I long for You.

Lord, take me to the next place with You ... the next high rock of Your calling.

Oh Father ... I cannot remain the wallflower ... let me dance with delight, full of the joy of knowing You.

Forever and ever. Amen.

When we are first learning to dance, it's always better to have someone to take you by the hand and whisper softly in your ear, "No worries; just watch me, follow my lead. I am going to teach you exactly what to do."

So That Your Soul Can Catch Up

Week 2

The Un-Woman

Remember last week and the inheritance of our salvation? Possibly one of the most mind-boggling of all the gifts God has given is His never-ending, lavish love for each one of us. Our holy God is passionately in love with His creation. I hope you always remember what a big deal His love is. And I hope we never get over being chosen by the Almighty, Creator of the Universe.

That kind of love means that no women are relegated to wallflower lives. Because of God's love for us, not one of us has to become the un-woman with the un-life. We do not have to numb down and go away. God has intended so much more for your life and mine.

Look at these words of Jesus with me:

I came to give life—life in all its fullness.
John 10:10, NCV

My seminary professor, Dr. Howard Hendricks, used to translate John 10:10 like this:

I came that you might live—and I mean really live!

You need to know that God's abundant, lavish, never-ending, pursuing love is for you! You still have the rest of your life to be lived—and I mean really lived! No woman who makes her life in Christ has to live empty.

Now here is the clincher … you can become distracted by your day-to-day life and lose sight of God's love. Did you know that you begin to believe what you focus on?

Most of us don't just wake up one morning and think to ourselves, *I am officially giving up on life. I am checking out. Numbing down. Going nowhere. Only breathing and surviving from here on out.* But for many of us, it happens anyway. Various degrees of giving up. Various degrees of an un-person with an un-life. Becoming an un-woman.

Maybe you've known Jesus for a very long time. But now, you still know Him but without very much passion. You may be looking for hope. Just getting by.

Daily Prayer Praise

Praise be to the Lord, to God our Savior, who daily bears our burdens.

Psalm 68:19

We know and rely on the love God has for us. God is love. Whoever lives in love lives in God and God in him.
1 John 4:16

We all know that life is big, and it just keeps coming to all of us. Disappointment. Rejection. Sadness. Struggle. Insecurity. Sickness. I am sure some kind of real life has bumped up against you lately. Just this week, I have dealt with a couple of difficult struggles. Actually, they were just little things, but they required several days of deep emotional conversations and truth telling to eventually reach resolution. But goodness, that little struggle with one person took it out of me.

Now, pile up decades of those small struggles for all of us, and the soul grows weary. Dreams fade. We can become numb, and many of us try to stay numb. Trying not to feel because feeling might hurt again.

I have been the un-woman, mostly on the inside where no one else could see. I'm sure you know, numb is not what God envisioned for either of us. The un-woman is not growing spiritually. She is just watching and getting by as best she can. A wallflower life with a wallflower heart.

How have you stopped becoming or maybe even given up over the years? Think about each one of these areas:

Your physical body:

Your spiritual relationship with God:

As I reflect on my own journey, I become more and more aware of how long I have played the role of observer. ... I had never fully given up the role of bystander. Even though there has been in me a lifelong desire to be an insider looking out, I nevertheless kept choosing over and over again the position of the outsider looking in.

—Henri Nouwen [1]

Your deeper relationships with friends and family:

Your self-improvement:

Sometimes a woman will tell me there is nothing wallflower about her life until she considers the condition of her heart. How is your heart with God today?

Wallflower	Wanting More	Growing	Dancing

As it turns out, I am not the only woman to ever give up and retreat into the barren life of a wallflower. I recognize that familiar emptiness in women everywhere I go. I sit beside women on airplanes. I look into their eyes at conferences. I live in their neighborhood, go to church with them, and wait in carpool lines with women who are, little by little, going away. Playing it safe. Blending in. Un-becoming.

Believe me, I get it. Depending on your circumstances, you may begin to feel giving in to nothingness or losing yourself in the chaos of busyness is the least painful option. More and more, it seems many women are surviving decades of their lives by turning their hearts inside out, trying not to feel. Becoming un-women.

A couple of years ago, I asked about 150 women, "Why aren't we becoming the women we have always wanted to be?" The theme that ran through their answers was amazing to me.

How would you answer that question? We aren't becoming the women we have always wanted to be because …

Almost every woman I asked listed *fear* in some form or fashion. So I began to pray to the Lord,

What if we could diminish fear in the hearts of women? What if we began to live and respond from courage? What if fear lost its grip and the wallflowers began to step out of the shadows? What if women could begin to live in righteous confidence?

What if women began to live just like the women God had always envisioned we would become? Godly. Righteous. Strong. Amazing. Confident.

Very clearly, God called me personally to grow up and never stop growing up in my salvation. I believe that call from His Word is the answer to our dilemma. Every one of us who has become a wallflower somewhere in her life can truly begin to dance! The key to this whole thing is the decision to grow up in your faith. To become a mature believer. And no matter where you are with God, deciding to take the next step higher. Closer. More of God and less of me. Moving away from my walls and toward the heart of my Savior. God is calling you today. Remember our verses from last week:

> *Like newborn babies, crave pure spiritual milk, so that by it you may grow up into your salvation, now that you have tasted that the Lord is good.*
> **1 Peter 2:2-3**

Last week we talked about coming to the altar of God with the truth of who we really are. This week is about really beginning to grow up in our faith. Deeper and higher. Enough of a wallflower life with God. Baby, it's time to dance!

Reflect on your faith now as compared to the faith you had 10 years ago.

How has your Bible-study time changed?

How have you changed in that same 10 years?

How has your view of God changed?

Is your relationship with God growing or standing still?

Pray with me something like this.

> *God, I want to crave You like a baby craves milk. Let these weeks be the beginning of spiritual growth in me. God, make this time like nothing I have ever experienced with You before. I want to be an amazing woman of Christ! I want to be everything You dreamed for me. I commit myself to Your truth and to know You more. God, I want to dance the dance of my life in Your arms. Please come and teach me. Have patience with me. Challenge me. Give me an eager heart.*
>
> *In Jesus' name, amen.*

Day 2

Choosing God

I do realize this sounds so basic.

So simple.

Like Jesus 101.

But the very first step toward spiritual growth is choosing with your heart and your mind that maturity is what you want.

Maybe you've tried many other things. You may have read books that promise to improve your potential, expand your mind, and increase your wealth. Maybe you've done a hundred other things in the desire to live a better life or become a better person. I believe that growing up in your faith, choosing God more than anything, is the most powerful and life-changing step you'll ever take.

So before we begin today, let's praise the One who is the answer.

Turning from the wallflower life and to the dance you were made for requires a choosing. Not choosing God means standing against the wall for the rest of your life.

Can you remember other significant times when you have chosen to pursue spiritual growth with God?

Maybe you decided to begin going to church or attending a Bible study. Maybe you decided to change your circle of friends or some habits that had kept you from God.

What happened in the past when you chose to grow in your faith?

Daily Prayer Praise

You alone are the LORD. You made the heavens, even the highest heavens, and all their starry host, the earth and all that is on it, the seas and all that is in them. You give life to everything, and the multitudes of heaven worship you.

Nehemiah 9:6

As you begin to think more about this intentional decision to choose God and greater spiritual maturity, what choices (big and little) can you begin to make toward growth?

For example, what if every night before you go to bed, you schedule a time with God? Think through tomorrow's schedule. When is the best time for you? It might be in the morning, at lunch, or at night. It doesn't have to be the same each day. But choosing a time will be an intentional decision to grow with Him each day.

What other intentional decisions can you make now that will encourage your intimacy with God?

1.

2.

3.

A Girlfriend Nudge

Make or buy a visual CHOOSING GOD reminder for yourself. I know that you're very creative, so make something you'll see every day to be a reminder you are choosing to grow in your faith. Maybe you can buy a beautiful candle that you light as a reminder. Maybe your visual will be a framed scrapbook page. I know you'll come up with something special that reminds you of God.

Read the following passage from *The Message*:

*No prolonged infancies among us, please. We'll not tolerate babes in the woods, small children who are an easy mark for impostors. God wants us to **grow up,** to know the whole truth and tell it in love—like Christ in everything. We take our lead from Christ, who is the source of everything we do. He keeps us in step with each other. His very breath and blood flow through us, nourishing us so that we will **grow up** healthy in God, robust in love.*
Ephesians 4:14-16, emphasis mine

What is Paul talking about in these verses?

How does this passage apply to you right now?

How does the fact that "His very breath and blood flow through us" make you feel?

Personally, I revise my spiritual goals through the years. Some are a little academic; I want to own so much more Bible knowledge. Some are intimate, deeper emotional interactions with the Lord. And some deal with practicing my faith both in ministry and family.

In what ways do you want to grow spiritually in this particular season of your life?

Academic:

Intimate:

Practicing:

I have said before that my personal, spiritual goal is that I would be a woman who eats, sleeps, drinks, and breathes Jesus. Of course, my humanity keeps me from such a perfect relationship, but it is a goal nonetheless.

Now, let's take this idea of spiritual goals one step further. What can you do today to accomplish those academic, intimate, and practicing spiritual goals?

Who do you want to be spiritually intentional for? For starters, I want to grow up in my faith to bless God and return to Him the love and devotion He has given to me. Then, I want to grow up for me. I have this burning desire not to miss anything. I don't want to miss the woman I could be if I pursue maturity. I want self-maturity for my children, the people I love, and the ministry God has given to me.

So what about you? Who do you want to grow up for?

I realize that you can choose God and mean to be intentional and then forget. So let's commit to whatever it takes to remember. Make your visual reminder. Write words of encouragement on your walls. Dangle a reminder from your rearview mirror. Anything that will remind you what you are choosing today.

Fill in the following with me:

Hey _____!
You are deciding today that you want to choose spiritual maturity. You want to grow up in your faith.

Today's date:

This is how you feel right now:

And here is the short prayer you prayed when you chose to be intentional about God:

OK, my friend. No matter what, keep reminding yourself that dancing with God is a deliberate choice of your heart. Keep choosing God!

Day 3

Stopping for a While

One day my friend, Dennis, phoned me and said, "I am going to tell you exactly what to do." You can imagine how it felt to have someone care so deeply and give this broken-down Jesus girl somewhere to start. I hope these weeks are like that for you. I want to tell you what God has done for me, kind of like passing my notes back, so that somehow, someway, your own spiritual growth is renewed with a fresh desire.

If we could have painted a picture of me during some of my darkest days, I would have been slumped over in the corner of my bedroom, in the dark, sucking my thumb. A pretty sad state of affairs. When God came to my rescue, it was as if He tenderly began to remind me of His love and call me deeper into His heart. It turned out that the steps toward His voice are steps toward spiritual maturity.

I want to take you where I have been and teach you as I have been taught. May God multiply each lesson and experience in your life for His glory.

In order to grow, maybe you need to stop for a while.

When God began to walk me out of that dark corner and into the light of His hope, one of the very first things He made clear with me was that I would have to stop many things in order to begin again my spiritual growth with Him. My body had outrun my soul. Read these great words by Gordon MacDonald:

> Study the life of Christ, and you will discover that He was never on the verge of passionlessness. He obviously understood how one gets into that kind of situation. It is no accident that before and after heavy periods of activity He went apart and stored up, or replenished, the inner energy or passion necessary to carry out His mission. And, again, it is no accident that He never seems to have engaged in activity that was beyond His reasonable limits. [2]

How does that description of Jesus' life differ from your own?

Daily Prayer Praise

Yet I am poor and needy;
come quickly to
me, O God.
You are my help and
my deliverer;
O LORD, do not delay.

Psalm 70:5

Discipleship—When one follower of Christ trains another follower in the truths he or she has learned.

Because we are pursuing Christ's filling, I think it's completely appropriate to stop long enough to begin this new journey of spiritual growth the right way. So I am going to ask you to stop for a while. I realize that you may be rolling your eyes at me, wondering who appointed me official world-stopper. No one, actually. I'm just telling you how God walked me out of 15 years of numb and back into my life.

So here you go:

(Note that I am leaving space after each suggestion so you can write down why you are sure you cannot do each one. I think it's probably better to go ahead and get it out, then we'll work on implementing in a minute.)

1. Only continue in the mandatory commitments necessary to care for your family and your career.

2. Complete any other time and energy obligations you have made, or determine an ending time for your open-ended "extra" obligations.

Note to single women:

I also decided that during this time I should not pursue an exclusive dating relationship. That was a personal decision based on the healing that needed to begin in my heart. I was afraid of choosing out of my emptiness. It may not apply to you, but at least stop for a moment and consider if God is speaking this same word to you.

3. Do not take on any new responsibilities for a determined length of time. (I really want you to seek God on the length of time. I feel that it should be extended and sufficient for restoration. Pray it through. Wait until you have heard God.)

4. Let the people in your life know that you are not accepting new obligations during this focused time of soul care.

You may have just decided that I have no concept of real life and that you cannot possibly stop doing anything. Or you may be the person in charge of recruiting Sunday School teachers and you are steamed at my suggestions.

I don't want to bring great catastrophe to your life. I just want you to recover your heart. So maybe you need to stop some of this craziness. Really. Don't wait until the kids are grown or until the pension kicks in. You could live your best life in Christ now.

Somewhere we've learned that it's wrong for us to focus on ourselves. It is wrong to become self-absorbed, egotistical, and narcissistic. But in order to grow, the un-woman has to stop and survey where she is and who she's become.

God gives you permission to get your life back, but stopping for a time should not hurt the people you love. This not about being distant in countenance or drawing difficult boundaries that keep others out. It's the distracting activity that needs to go away for a while. You will actually need other people more than ever.

What three things that you could stop quickly come to mind?

1.

2.

3.

Now just to stretch yourself, add two more:

4.

5.

I believe this really matters. You will have plenty of time to be room mom and first-base coach and city council advocate later. Actually, you may even enjoy all of those things even more after you have stepped back to locate your heart.

So let's end this day with prayer. Ask God these things:

Do you want me to stop extra activities for a while?

Please tell me exactly what needs to be set aside.

How long should this focused time last?

Please encourage my family to accept my decisions.

Stress is when your gut says, "No," but your mouth says, "Of course, I'd be glad to."

A Girlfriend Nudge

Memorize Psalm 46.

This has been a big idea thrown at you in a short space. Hold this idea in your heart and listen for God to lead.

Day 4

Meeting Together

Daily Prayer Praise

Praise be to the God and Father of our Lord Jesus Christ, the Father of compassion and the God of all comfort.

2 Corinthians 1:3

As you become increasingly more intentional about growing up in your faith, we cannot diminish an important principle of Scripture. Read Hebrews 10:25.

Let us not give up meeting together, as some are in the habit of doing, but let us encourage one another—and all the more as you see the Day approaching.

Yesterday I asked you to stop spinning for a while so that you might focus on your spiritual growth. But that does not mean turning away from love, companionship, or the body of Christ. Meeting and being together is one of the most powerful tools God will use to refill your heart and bring your soul back to life.

I do not know of one person who has ever been healed by crying alone on her bed in the dark. Every person I know who finds healing for his or her wounds or strength to battle addictions or sin finds it in the light of fellowship and love.

Remember a time of personal healing in your past. How did healing come to you?

Read what James Friesen, author of *Living from the Heart Jesus Gave You*, has to say:

Becoming mature requires bonds between people—they are the foundation upon which maturity is built. Bonds are the connections that energize us, motivate our actions and establish our identities. The receiving-and-giving exchange in our bonds shapes our view of what really is important.

He goes on:

> Love bonds ... motivate us to remain faithful under pressure, to help others to be all they were created to be, to be willing to endure pain in order to be close to those we love, and to tell the truth even when it hurts. [3]

To grow up in your faith, you need to continue in relationship and interacting. As simply as I can say it, the first place you need to be in relationship is your church. God inhabits the praise of His people, and you need to get in on that. God has promised that He will always use His church as an instrument of blessing, healing, and a place where He will abide.

Marathoners pace themselves according to those they run beside. Spiritual growth is the same. You will pace yourself according to those you run beside. Take a minute to think about the people you are pacing with spiritually.

Put a check beside the statement that most closely matches where you are:

- ☐ Still getting ready to think about running toward God.
- ☐ Back in the slow pack.
- ☐ Steady but not challenged.
- ☐ Running beside some people who cause me to pick up the pace.
- ☐ Scared out of my mind but more alive than I could ever imagine.

For a woman who has decided to take the next steps higher in her faith, the people with whom you meet could make all the difference. You want to be with other women who are thirsty for God. People who want to imitate Jesus. Learn more about giving and receiving grace.

> The people with whom you meet could make all the difference. You want to be with other women who are thirsty for God.

What areas of spiritual growth excite you right now?

Are you in a relationship(s) or place that is challenging you spiritually?

Specifically, who in your life could you begin to pace your spiritual life beside?

I want to take a few minutes to deal with a tough church issue. *Some of you have been wounded in the very place where you should have been loved.* I want you to know that a healthy church should not be a dangerous place to confess your sin and find help for your brokenness. Church is a safe place to encounter God. If you do not attend a safe place, find one. The responsibility to connect to a healthy body of believers is on you. You have to make the effort to find your way into a healthy, fairly functional fellowship of believers. No church is perfect, but healthy churches do exist.

Now take a little personal church inventory:

A Girlfriend Nudge

You knew it was coming. It's time to memorize the Old Testament books in order. Quick, run down to the children's department at your church. I'm sure they have a song somewhere that will teach you all the books along with a catchy tune!

I attend a church where the pastor opens the Bible and teaches from the Scriptures.
☐ yes ☐ no ☐ sometimes

The leadership of my church is respected for its integrity and spiritual desire.
☐ yes ☐ no ☐ sometimes

I take my Bible to church.
☐ yes ☐ no ☐ sometimes

I take notes in a journal because I am expecting God to say something important to me.
☐ yes ☐ no ☐ sometimes

I listen to the sermon and ask God how I can apply the lessons to my life.
☐ yes ☐ no ☐ sometimes

I sing during worship.
☐ yes ☐ no ☐ sometimes

I am willing to walk down front and let people pray for me.
☐ yes ☐ no ☐ sometimes

I am connected to some people from my church. They know my name and care for my life.
☐ yes ☐ no ☐ sometimes

Now look at your responses. Are you really meeting together with the body of Christ?

By way of reminder, let's look at a few of the blessings that happen when you meet together with the body of Christ:

> *Carry each other's burdens, and in this way you will fulfill the law of Christ.*
> **Galatians 6:2**

> *Therefore confess your sins to each other and pray for each other so that you may be healed. The prayer of a righteous man is powerful and effective.*
> **James 5:16**

> *Where two or three come together in my name, there am I with them.*
> **Matthew 18:20**

I know that you know this, but the church is made up of people just like you. They all need a Savior. Come to them as you would have them come to you, full of grace and mercy, mindful of the forgiveness you have received from Jesus. Ready to give to them what has already been given in your inheritance.

Day 5

Restoring Order

I can't think when things are messy. Really, I have this whole little ritual thing I go through before I can actually sit down and write. I read the paper and fold a load of clothes. Organize the stacks on my desk. Read my Bible. Write in my journal. Go upstairs and brush my teeth again. Look at my calendar. Work on my to-do list. It's a version of piddling and connecting the dots that actually gets me over into thinking and making the

Daily Prayer Praise

God is able to make all grace abound to you, so that in all things at all times, having all that you need, you will abound in every good work.

2 Corinthians 9:8

words happen. It feels as if I have to get my arms around my life every morning and then I can take the next few steps.

In much the same way, I believe we have to get our arms around the bigger picture of our lives before we can take the next steps of growth. As we begin today's study, I believe the essential first work will involve restoring order to your daily life, both to your physical home and your physical body.

I talked to a woman a few months ago who had gotten herself into some of the biggest life messes you can imagine. She was literally losing everything, all at the same time. She couldn't think or even begin to start untangling the wreckage she had caused. She said, "Angela my whole life is a mess. I don't even have any clean clothes, and I haven't paid the bills, and the sink is full of dirty dishes." As you already know, all that overwhelming, outward disorder is a direct reflection into the soul.

I asked her, "What can you go home and do right now?"

She said, "I could do the laundry."

"Start there," I offered. "Begin to restore some physical order so that you can think."

Maybe you aren't facing the same huge mess as that woman, but places in your life need order restored so you can be free to grow. You may need to start small and just do what you can, as you can. That's where I was for months. I remember when cleaning out my purse was an accomplishment. If your outside world has grown to reflect your inside chaos, I am asking you to begin to revive the place where you live. Reorder your belongings. Brighten up your surroundings. Just a clean, orderly home will give you such a fresh spirit.

So, what can you do first? Choose just one.

- ☐ Sort out the garage or your closet.
- ☐ Give away some clutter or just have the junk hauled off.
- ☐ Balance your checkbook and recommit to a financial budget.
- ☐ Mow the lawn or weed the flower bed.
- ☐ Find the top of your washer and dryer. Then put all that stuff where it belongs.
- ☐ Clean out your car.

What makes the top of your restoring order list?

You might be thinking to yourself, *I thought we were talking about spiritual maturity.* We are. But if the foundational structure of your life is in chaos and disrepair, we have nowhere to build.

Maybe restoring order for you would mean giving yourself more time to think. Maybe you need to turn down the constant, repetitive noise in your life. Turn off the TV. Take at least one day a week without your cell phone. Don't check your e-mail all weekend.

Ask God, Where does my life need more stability and rearranging?

As you pray, I am sure God will direct. Ask God, *Where does my life need more stability and rearranging?*

I know you don't want me to bring it up, but I have to. We cannot begin to restore order to our everyday lives without talking about restoring order to our physical bodies. The truth is that our body and emotions are so intricately intertwined that I cannot speak to your soul without directing you to give attention to your body.

Emotional health feeds physical health.
   Physical health feeds emotional health.
      And then our spiritual health reflects the
      mind, body, and soul working together.

A part of realizing our potential as godly women means deciding to care for our bodies as they were meant to be cared for.

I love this exhortation to you and to me:

> Didn't you realize that your body is a sacred place, the place of the Holy Spirit? Don't you see that you can't live however you please, squandering what God paid such a high price for? The physical part of you is not some piece of property belonging to the spiritual part of you. God owns the whole works. So let people see God in and through your body.
> **1 Corinthians 6:19-20, MSG**

One thing I have realized in past years is that I need a stronger body to live the life God is calling me to. A million great ideas float around out there about how to restore your body. But here is my best advice for getting started. Go anyway.

We could spend a two-hour lunch exchanging all the reasons we do not have time or inclination. Go anyway. The kids might smirk. Go anyway. Your husband might look at you like you're cross-eyed. Go anyway. Your workout clothes might feel too tight. Go anyway. You might not have any hope that this time you'll stick to it. Go anyway.

Spend some time praying about how to care for your body.

I can tell you that I began working out in earnest about four years ago. This past year, everything caved in, and I stopped going to the gym for at least six months. I gained 15 pounds and felt awful. I have been back in my routine of going to the gym for two months, and once again I am reminded that I cannot ever stop taking care of my body again. Even though the pounds will take a while to get off, my spirit soars after an hour of doing the very thing I always dread.

Restoring order. It will require a continued choosing. We want to live differently. We want to grow up in our faith. Things will have to change to make way for growth. So, go girl! Tackle that messy closet. Walk around the neighborhood. You can do it!

1. Henri J. M. Nouwen, *The Return of the Prodigal Son* (New York: Image Books, 1994), 12.

2. Gordon MacDonald, Restoring Your Spiritual Passion (Nashville: Oliver Nelson, 1986), 34.

3. James G. Friesen et al., Living from the Heart Jesus Gave You (Pasadena, CA: Shepherd's House, 2000), 16.

Prayer

My sweet Father in heaven,

I come to You this week so very grateful for Your love. I keep remembering the riches of my salvation and I rejoice over Your goodness to me. Your love is amazing.

This week I am asking You to prompt my heart every time You have something new for me to see. Do whatever You must to get my attention. Make me aware of my own patterns. Unveil my eyes. Let me see my life as You see it.

But more than anything, please be the Shepherd who restores my soul.

I love You. I desire the fullness of life that You bring.

I am Your baby girl.

Amen

With a clean life and a clear conscience, the wallflower can lift up her head and look intently into the eyes of the One who has asked her to dance.

A Clean Life

Week 3

A Clear Conscience

Let's begin with our commitment to daily praise!

Several years ago, I probably thought that I was a very mature Christ-follower. And in many ways I was. Knowledgeable. Committed. Faithful. Passionate. Unwavering. But what I didn't fully realize was that the growth potential with God is without end. No matter my age or how long I have walked with God, I am called to keep growing in wisdom. Keep pursuing deeper truths. Keep stepping up to the next high place with God. The adventure of keeping on with God is very exciting to me. I want each maturity lesson that God brings to radically impact my life and keep changing me into His likeness.

This week we'll consider a very powerful God-lesson. I am praying that its importance will at the same time bring freedom and guardrails to your spiritual life. Would you pray with me and ask God to take this week down deep into your soul?

Before we jump into this week's lesson, think back about some of the God-lessons you have been taught. What are the first three that come to mind?

1.

2.

3.

Almost everywhere I go and in lots of the interviews I do, people ask me the same question: "How do you do everything? How do you take care of the children, write, and speak?" I used to say, "I fly by the seat of my pants. Somehow it all comes together and God takes care of us."

I have walked with God for at least 25 years, but after being asked the same question so many times, I began to ask myself: *What is making the past years different and stronger even though I*

Daily Prayer Praise

Praise the LORD, O my
*   soul;*
*   all my inmost being,*
*   praise his holy*
*   name.*
Praise the LORD, O my
*   soul,*
*   and forget not all his*
*   benefits—*
who forgives all your sins
*   and heals all your*
*   diseases,*
who redeems your life
*   from the pit*
*   and crowns you*
*   with love and*
*   compassion.*

Psalm 103:1-4

have known more brokenness, pain, and seeming attack than ever? Why am I more profoundly assured of God's presence, unlike any other season of my life? How am I making it?

The truth of God's provision came to me through one particular passage of Scripture. Turn in your Bible to 2 Timothy 1:3,6-7.

*I thank God, whom I serve, as my forefathers did, with **a clear conscience,** as night and day I constantly remember you in my prayers. For this reason I remind you to fan into flame the gift of God, which is in you through the laying on of my hands. For God did not give us **a spirit of timidity, but a spirit of power, of love and of self-discipline.***
(emphasis mine)

In this book, the apostle Paul wrote Timothy from a prison cell. Paul had been discipling Timothy in the faith, and the two letters Paul wrote to him are for continued training, encouragement, and growth.

The first thing I want you to see if the little phrase in verse 3, "a clear conscience." Paul built the rest of his letter on this truth: his conscience was clear. Let's take a moment to remember who Paul had been before he met Jesus on the road to Damascus.

Before his conversion, Paul was called Saul. In Acts 9:1 it says, "Saul was still breathing out murderous threats against the Lord's disciples. He went to the high priest ... so that if he found any [in Damascus] who belonged to the Way, whether men or women, he might take them as prisoners to Jerusalem."

Tomorrow we'll talk about how Paul received a clear conscience, but today I want you to see the immense value of knowing your conscience is clean. It will add power to your life.

When Paul wrote his second letter to Timothy, he had lived many faithful years following Christ's teachings. He could tell Timothy that his conscience was clear, and he could model how to live a faithful life with a clear conscience. It's obvious from many of Paul's writings that a clear conscience was a vital part of his serving God.

I believe Paul wanted Christ-followers to understand the importance of living clean and to pursue a clear conscience as both necessary and desirable. Its presence in our lives begins to make a way for our gifts to fan into flame so that we might operate in the Spirit of Power Paul wrote about in 2 Timothy 1:7.

Where do you fall on the "Spirit of Power" scale?

Spirit of Timidity   **Spirit of Power**

I believe that we live as timid women when we operate in the flesh, giving preference to our fears, dallying with secret sin, harboring bitterness or a grudge, or living without self-discipline. The causes of timidity are as varied as the personalities we uniquely possess. But God gives the gift of power to the woman growing in her faith, cleaning up her heart and mind—the one who is living clean.

Spiritual power comes into our lives—or is withheld—for many reasons. But this week, the very first place I want you to look is into your own heart and conscience. Begin to ask the Lord to show you the answer to these questions:

Am I clean before God?

Is my conscience clear?

As you pray the next few days, ask the Lord, "Is there anything that would make me unclean?"

Keep this in my mind as you pray. My friend Mark Pate says there are two types of sin:

1. Not obeying, which is the sin of rebellion; and

2. the sin of presumption, which is going ahead when God has not issued a directive, which always has consequences.

Sometimes we are slow to hear God's promptings and then many of us are even slower to respond. My prayer is that by the end of this week, you will be clean before the Lord and He will bless your faithfulness with the promised Spirit of Power that Paul offered to Timothy.

*Keep a **clear conscience** before God so that when people throw mud at you, none of it will stick. They'll end up realizing that they're the ones who need a bath.*
1 Peter 3:16, MSG (emphasis mine)

Day 2

God Makes You Clean

Daily Prayer Praise

If we confess our sins, he is faithful and just and will forgive us our sins and purify us from all unrighteousness.

1 John 1:9

Many of us find the idea of living a clean life or keeping a clear conscience almost impossible. Maybe your choices have been downright awful and you are sure that you stand in front of God, dirty and repulsive to His holiness. Maybe no one in the room would ever guess what you have hidden and the ugliness you try to keep them from knowing.

The age-old problem of an unclean life keeps us from an intimacy with God, and it also keeps us from living in the power He wants us to enjoy. I believe that a central lesson to growing up in our faith is deciding to respond to the call to live a clean life.

Before you feel beat up or overwhelmed, I want us to take a few minutes looking at the man the apostle Paul had been. He persecuted Christians and had a goal to destroy anyone associated with the Way of Jesus:

> But Saul [Paul] began to destroy the church. Going from house to house, he dragged off men and women and put them in prison.
> **Acts 8:3**

> I'm sure that you've heard the story of my earlier life when I lived in the Jewish way. In those days I went all out in persecuting God's church. I was systematically destroying it.
> **Galatians 1:14, MSG**

Paul had really been a bad guy. And it wasn't just that he slipped up a few times; he had intentionally chosen wicked, sinful ways.

I know it's a fairly long passage, but read the conversion story about Saul (who later became Paul) in Acts 9:1-22, and answer the following:

Whom does Saul encounter on his journey to Damascus?

What did the Lord ask Saul in verse 4?

Note that Jesus asks, "Why do you persecute Me?" The reference to "Me" gave Saul his first glimpse into the doctrine of Christians being in Christ. We are the body of Christ on earth.

What did Ananias call Saul in verse 17?

Can you imagine what it felt like for Paul to be called "brother" for the very first time? Saul dramatically met Jesus on the road. Sometime between that moment and when the scales fell from his eyes in verse 18, Saul believed in the One he had spent his life denying and attacking. In that moment of belief, Jesus made Saul clean.

What did Saul begin to do in verse 20?

Grab hold to this today: a clear conscience and a clean life come from the goodness of God and are available to anyone who seeks to follow Jesus … even a person who had lived a despicable life like Paul.

Now back to you and me. Most likely, you are not a despicable woman. I haven't ever chosen anything despicable, but I have been unclean before God. I have learned that when I am unclean I live and act with a spirit of timidity. Have you ever seen this in someone around you? They begin to act distant, weird, aloof. You wonder what's wrong. They say, "Nothing." But everything feels off-kilter. Sure enough, some time goes by, the truth comes out, and the distant friend had been trying to keep something in the dark: a sin, an action, or a poor choice.

Why do you suppose we become timid when we're not dealing with our sin?

Here's what I know from both personal experience and observation: if your conscience is not clear, then you spend a lot of mental and emotional energy trying to cover things up. The murky conscience requires a great deal of thinking devoted to inner wrangling and rationalizing. A burdened conscience is a heavy chain that keeps you shackled to a wall of guilt and never lets you get very far. All along God intended for us to dance.

Read again our praise verse for today on page 50. Rewrite it here, substituting "I" and "me" for "we" and "us."

A Girlfriend Nudge

Confess your sin … out loud.

My out-loud time with God usually happens in the car when I'm driving alone. Something is more powerful about asking for God's forgiveness out loud. You speak the depth of your heart and you receive the treasure of God's forgiveness.

Here is the great, great news. Jesus Christ is the One who makes you clean. He is the one who clears your conscience. He made a despicable man like Saul into a powerful display of God's glory. Even so, Christ delights in making you into a righteous woman with a clear conscience and a clean life.

Take time right now to intentionally ask God to make you clean. Spend some time with God however you feel led … pray on your face, journal, bow your head, or take a walk. Spend however long God leads you, but ask … ask to be made clean.

We live in such a dark society that I think we've come to accept our society's darkness as an unavoidable part of our own. It can begin to feel as if we are required to pull a ball and chain of guilt and private struggle around with us. Besides, it seems everybody else does. But it does not have to be so.

Psalm 38:4 tells us, "You know my folly, O God; my guilt is not hidden from you." He already knows everything we've done.

We belong to God, and He has made a way for us to live in the light. We can live with a clear conscience because of the freedom Christ gives. We can pursue a clean life even if no one else around us wants to go there, and even if others continue to remind us of our mistakes. We do not have to be shackled to guilt and the shame of poor choices for a lifetime. Because of Jesus, we can serve God with a clear conscience.

What does it mean to you that Christ became the guilt offering for us (Isa. 53:10)?

No matter what is in our past, Christ has carried our guilt. That is a truth that will allow you to sleep like a baby!

Day 3

God's Forgiveness

Did you know that when God forgives, He intends for that forgiveness to wipe our slate clean *and* free us from our guilt?

Being free of guilt is possibly one of God's most difficult next-level truths for me to personally receive and apply. All the time God has been yelling to me, "I want to set you free! I want to make you clean. I'm sending a Savior. I am moving heaven and earth to get to you." And for most of my life I have rejected this kind of freedom from guilt.

Daily Prayer Praise

They refused to listen and failed to remember the miracles you performed among them. They became stiff-necked and in their rebellion appointed a leader in order to return to their slavery. But you are a forgiving God, gracious and compassionate, slow to anger and abounding in love. Therefore you did not desert them.

Nehemiah 9:17

How do you deal with guilt?

☐ I'm still carrying around guilt from kindergarten.
☐ I've let go of the little things but still haul around the biggies.
☐ I try to lay down my guilt but the people in my life are great guilt-reminders.
☐ I'm free! It's a gift from God I still can't understand but I really do celebrate His goodness and forgiveness toward me.

Most of my life, guilt somehow seemed righteous. In my immaturity, I believed if I kept flogging myself before God, He'd be happier with me because of my shame. Good grief, how misled we can be.

Come to find out, most women feel much the same way and struggle with the application of this truth. Not long ago a woman asked to have breakfast with me. She was single and had allowed herself to act inappropriately with a man she had been dating. She was brokenhearted over her mistake, and we sat together and sorted things out. She was mad at herself, frustrated by her poor choices, and aching over her shame before the man and before God. We talked through her obvious repentance, prayed together, and I am sure that she received God's complete forgiveness that morning.

About eight months later she came to me again, still grieving the same sin of that one night. Still flogging herself.

"Has anything happened since we last talked?" I asked. "Have you made similar choices again? Has that night become a pattern for you in any way?"

"No," she spoke through her tears. "It was just that one time, but I still live with such shame and regret. I'm reminded all the time of my blatant disobedience to God."

"Do you remember the morning that we prayed and asked God for His forgiveness?" I asked.

She nodded her head that she remembered.

"Then tell me what we have if the forgiveness of God does not truly forgive."

My friend said nothing.

"Look at me," I gently persuaded. "You have been forgiven. Your conscience is clear. The Accuser wants you to live in shame and weakness because of your mistake. Eight months have gone by and you could have been living grateful for the forgiveness God has given. It's time to lift your head up. God has made you clean."

Do you ever suffer with continued guilt even after you have earnestly asked God for forgiveness? ☐ yes ☐ no

Why do we so easily slip into chronic self-punishment through persisting guilt? Record your thoughts here.

Let's look at the following passage together:

> Who is a God like you,
> > who pardons sin and forgives the transgression
> > of the remnant of his inheritance?
> > You do not stay angry forever
> > but delight to show mercy.
> You will again have compassion on us;
> > you will tread our sins underfoot
> > and hurl all our iniquities into the depths of the sea.
>
> **Micah 7:18-19**

This is one of my all-time favorite passages. Before we jump in, reread this same passage in *The Message* paraphrase:

> Where is the god who can compare with you—
> > wiping the slate clean of guilt,
> Turning a blind eye, a deaf ear,
> > to the past sins of your purged and precious people?
> You don't nurse your anger and don't stay angry long,
> > for mercy is your specialty. That's what you love most.
> And compassion is on its way to us.
> > You'll stamp out our wrongdoing.
> You'll sink our sins
> > to the bottom of the ocean.

Now let's answer these questions together:

What does God do with our sin?

Is He angry about having to forgive you of your sin? ☐ yes ☐ no

In fact, according to the first translation, how does God feel about showing mercy?

And where exactly does God put our sin?

A long time ago, I heard someone say that God sinks our sin to the bottom of the ocean and then posts a "NO FISHING" sign.

Do you still "go fishing" for old sins? ☐ yes ☐ no

What in your life can trigger the "fishing trip" for old guilt?

Here's how I have come to feel about the pursuit of a clear conscience. Either the forgiveness that God has promised to us is half-hearted, based on some unattainable, unknown standard of self-flogging and sustained guilt, or His forgiveness really forgives—instantly, eternally, and completely.

Either I believe that forgiveness is what God said—free, available to any who would call on His name, and completely able to cleanse the impure heart—or I don't really believe God. Either God can make you clean or He is not God.

> Either I believe that forgiveness is what God said—free, available to any who would call on His name, and completely able to cleanse the impure heart—or I don't really believe God.

I am staking my whole life on the belief that God is who He says He is. Jesus is really His Son, my Savior. His death was enough to pay the penalty for every sin. His resurrection was the proof of His divinity. The Holy Spirit is His promised gift to you and me for day-by-day, moment-to-moment guidance.

And for some reason, that doesn't make sense to anybody. God is so crazy in love with His creation that He freely forgives any who ask. In case you haven't thought about it lately, when the God of heaven and earth forgives, nothing can happen to make it less, and nothing you can do will make it more. Forgiven in the name of Jesus means your conscience is clear.

The Battle We Forget

In case you haven't thought about it in a while, I want to remind you that growing up, living a clean life, and becoming a mature woman of God is a spiritual battle. Satan absolutely does not want you to have a clear conscience or a clean life. He does not want your growth to happen. If you are running after God, then I can assure you there's a big red target on your back.

I know this might sound crazy, but for many years a spiritual battle was the last thing I would think of. I would forget that Satan wants my mind and my heart. He wants me to remain in emptiness or feel numb and overwhelmed. He wants to destroy my passion and kill every dream God has given to me. He wants my children. He wants to sneak into our home. He wants the presence of evil to begin to feel normal to us. He cannot have my soul, but he will settle for my life.

What does the statement mean to you that the life of a godly woman is a target for Satan?

What lies has Satan told you during this study?

On some days the determination to live a clean life and keep a clear conscience will require us to stand against Satan and his evil.

What is your most recent spiritual battle?

Daily Prayer Praise

The God of peace will soon crush Satan under your feet. The grace of our Lord Jesus be with you.

Romans 16:20

We bring a battle on ourselves when we choose to live unclean lives, shackled to sin. But the battle we're talking about today is for the woman who knows she has been made clean by God's forgiveness.

Sometimes I walk out of a meeting or away from a personal encounter feeling so discouraged. The numbers might indicate that business isn't going well. The next steps in a relationship aren't always clear. The input from others can seem muddled or confusing. It's uncomfortable to be deflated and still have to face conflict or decisions. It always makes me want to give up and run away. But eventually I will begin to hear this list of questions running through my head:

> *The devil … was a murderer from the beginning, not holding to the truth, for there is no truth in him. When he lies, he speaks his native language, for he is a liar and the father of lies.*
>
> **John 8:44**

Do you love God?	Yes.
Do you want to honor Him with your life?	Yes.
Are you living clean?	Yes.
Is your conscience clear?	Yes.

When all those answers are "yes," then I know what to do:

Get back in there and fight for goodness until you see the glory of God.

We fight the good fight so that the glory of God can be revealed, both in our personal lives and in the public testimony of our faith. I believe a huge piece of the good fight goes to this idea of a clear conscience and a clean life.

Who can have you when you are clean? No one. They can accuse you. They can gossip about you. Plans can fail. But when your heart is good and everything is on the table, out in the light, then God prevails. He can use a woman like that. He will be glorified in her.

Sometimes when I get to a speaking engagement, the ladies will tell me about all the things that have gone wrong in preparation for the conference. Crazy things. Sickness. Marital difficulty. Catering issues. Distracting and discouraging kinds of things. Almost every time, the woman's ministry leader will say something like this, "We believe this weekend is going to be powerful and anointed because the spiritual battle during our preparation has been intense. We called our prayer team and asked them to pray harder."

Personally, you should know that my life always blows apart, and I mean a really big explosion, when I am writing. My assistant dreads every new book's beginning. She moans, "Do you have to do that again?" because we know the always-present battle will begin to rage while I study and try to focus on a new message. Before I begin, we send e-mails to my prayer team and ask them to join us by praying for God's protection. It's a pattern we've finally come to recognize. At least in seeing Satan for the calculated serpent he really is, we are able to prepare and pray more effectively.

What spiritual battle patterns do you see in your life?

What current situation in your life may be a battle that needs to be fought in the heavenlies?

> *I am afraid that just as Eve was deceived by the serpent's cunning, your minds may somehow be led astray from your sincere and pure devotion to Christ.*
> **2 Corinthians 11:3**

You see, when you know you are clean before God, your conscience is clear, and everything still blows apart, then we know exactly what to do: get down on our knees and ask for heavenly protection and strength.

What can you do to prepare and respond effectively to spiritual battle?

Look at the truth of where you can turn and who powerfully fights for you:

> *The eternal **God** is your **refuge,** and underneath are the everlasting arms. He will drive out your enemy before you, saying, "Destroy him!"*
> **Deuteronomy 33:27, emphasis mine**

> *But as for me, the nearness of God is my good;*
> *I have made the Lord GOD my refuge,*
> *That I may tell of all Your works.*
> **Psalm 73:28, NASB**

What does the Lord provide for the woman who runs to His refuge?

Let's pray in two parts:

1. A plea for God's refuge specifically for your personal situation.
2. A thankful prayer for God's faithfulness and protection.

Stay safe in His everlasting arms today! I will see you tomorrow.

Day 5

No More Shackles

Daily Prayer Praise

Before they call I will answer;
   while they are still speaking I will hear.

Isaiah 65:24

Every weekend I talk to women who want to go forward personally, or in their marriage, but they find they can't. I usually ask some basic questions such as:

☐ Is your heart clean before God?
☐ Is your conscience clear?
☐ Have you done what you need to do to make things right?
☐ Have you done the work of receiving forgiveness?

I'm always surprised that women will many times respond, "No." They had wanted me to say something that lets them skip this part, but I can't. God calls us to live clean.

Maybe you wanted to skip this whole week too. But the lesson is so pivotal for spiritual growth that there are really no options for the woman who wants to run passionately after God and His will for her life. Remember these beautiful words of Jesus:

So if the Son sets you free, you will be free indeed.
John 8:36

We aspire to the truth that Jesus died so that we can live free! Both in this life and forever. Godly women are free of shackles and guilt. They are free to run with abandon toward their calling in Christ.

We can love freely because we are free.
We can forgive quickly because we are free.
We can pursue our dreams because we are free.

Free! Right there in your same old house and your same old job and your same old family, Jesus Christ wants to break the shackles that have held you down for so long.

So what will you choose?
Continued chains or the freedom to dance?

Maybe your conscience is not clear or you find yourself trapped inside a private world that is out of control or out of order. Maybe you aren't sure that you have ever stood clean before God. If you believe that you still live in shackles, here's what I want you to do. And even if you're without shackles, the following is good practice.

Begin by reading the following verses from the Bible. Listen to God affirm His desire that we live with a clear conscience.

I strive always to keep my conscience clear before God and man.
Acts 24:16

Now this is our boast: Our conscience testifies that we have conducted ourselves in the world, and especially in our relations with you, in the holiness and sincerity that are from God. We have done so not according to worldly wisdom but according to God's grace.
2 Corinthians 1:12

How much more is done by the blood of Christ. He offered himself through the eternal Spirit as a perfect sacrifice to God. His blood will make our consciences pure from useless acts so we may serve the living God.
Hebrews 9:14, NCV

Next is the choice to surrender to the process of being made clean. I realize this is probably uncomfortable for you. Nobody wants to have her bedroom door taken off its hinges. But sometimes it's necessary for a season in order to learn how to live when the door is returned.

---

1. Begin with self-examination.

Where are you with God today? What stands between you and a clear conscience? If you begin to peel back layers of patterns and habits you've developed over the years, will you find sin that you've hidden or covered?

2. Confess your sin.

Private confession applies to private sins. Public sins call for public confession. All sin is confessed to God. Private confession happens one-on-one with the one you offended or hurt. You may need a counselor or pastor who can maintain confidentiality for private confession. Private confession of private sin needs to remain private.

Public confession is required when your disobedience has publicly caused harm to others and to your reputation. For example, the newspaper journalist who has lied in her published reporting would not just confess to her editor. She must confess publicly.

I went through a time when I felt split open from head to toe. I remember begging God to show me anything else I needed to confess. While we were digging under my pretending, I asked Him to go even deeper and show me anything and everything that kept me from Him. When I am in my private time of confession with God, no reason should hold me back. I want to be clean, and this process is the only way to get there.

John Ortberg said that, "Confession is not just naming what we have done in the past. It involves our intentions about the future as well. It requires a kind of promise." [1]

3. Ask for forgiveness.

To confess is one step, but the humbling that comes in asking God's forgiveness is an act of obedience that cleanses. To ask for what we do not deserve also becomes a mile marker of sorts. One that reminds me of where I don't want to go again.

4. Receive God's mercy.

God delights to show mercy. He delights to hold back what you and I deserve. Receive this gift with gratefulness. God's mercy redeems your life. Listen to the truth of these words and their promise for your life:

> Redemption is God bringing good out of bad, leading us to wholeness, and the experience of God's amazing power. *Redemption means that out of our greatest pain, can come our most profound personal mission in life.* [2]

God's mercy redeems your life.

God can take your confession and do the amazing work of redemption. He can make your life clean and then give purpose to your personal mission. But for all that to happen, things really do have to change.

You and I can't stay in the old patterns of deceit and expect to live pure. We can't hang out with the people who led us down wrong paths. We can't visit the same old places anymore. We have to choose light over darkness and have nothing to do with the one who can lure us back with the same old tricks. If it feels like darkness, then it probably is. Choose the light.

We remain unclean because we don't want to stay surrendered to examination, confession, and forgiveness. I understand. It's one of the hardest and best things I do.

This day, run into the arms of God. Pray for His tender guidance. Ask Him for a clear conscience and let Him make you clean. Writer a prayer to Him here, confessing as you need in order to cleanse your conscience. Then receive forgiveness from your Heavenly Father!

1. John Ortberg, *The Life You've Always Wanted* (Grand Rapids, MI: Zondervan, 1997), 130.

2. James Friesen et. al., *Living from the Heart Jesus Gave You* (Pasadena, CA: Shepherd's House, 1999), 7-8.

Prayer

Father,

Use this week's biblical teaching in my mind and in my soul to make me clean. Reveal all my impurity. Uncover any secrets. Oh, Lord, please come to me with Your cleansing forgiveness. Order my steps according to Your will. Re-direct every wayward choice. Clean me up, oh God, and make my conscience clean.

God, I submit to this week because I know that You are tender and loving. Your best for me is what I desire. I want to live in righteousness. Please add Your power to my life. Make me amazing and godly and good like You.

Be merciful to me. I surrender to Your love.

Amen.

The bitter wallflower can only focus on the life she's never known and the parties she missed. The woman who resists bitterness and believes God is finally ready to dance.

Resisting Bitterness

Week 4

Day 1

A Hundred Reasons

As I became a young adult, I remember meeting people and wondering why so many were mad or sad or gloomy. It didn't take me long to find out. They had been hurt, abandoned, or rejected and the pain just never went away. Some of them wanted to leave the pain, but then it came again another way. Year after year, hurt after hurt, and the once-tender heart had grown bitter.

Probably every person I know could come up with about a hundred reasons to become bitter and remain a perpetually downtrodden victim. Remember Grayson's crackers from our video session? Most women have a lot more than a missing snack to make them sad. Real-life tragedies have come to them, or they've suffered awful consequence, more than one person should have to carry. So much disappointment and heartache. And I have my own list of a hundred reasons to become bitter. It could start somewhere with single mom-ness and end with bill-paying, yard-mowing, lonely-night frustration.

Hear me in this. I would be the first in line to give you permission to feel pain over your circumstances, disappointment, or anger. We cannot deny the pain so many of us have known. Life turns out rotten sometimes and to teach any different would be ridiculous. To act as if we can pretend our heartache away is even worse.

I think we give up because we can't see God working all things together for good. We fall into whining and complaining because we don't believe His promises are true. We cry, "Woe is me!" because we can't hear His voice anymore. Besides, living as a victim actually gets some os uf a little sympathy along the way and bitterness becomes more attractive the more empty we become.

Steve Brown wrote:

Bitterness comes from our turning away from the true God ... Bitterness—characterized by feelings of hatred, envy, resentment, cynicism, and severity—begins when one turns from God, and it results in a disease that infects others. [1]

Daily Prayer Praise

I am God your healer.

Exodus 15:26, MSG

Each heart knows its own bitterness.
Proverbs 14:10

How does bitterness show up in your life?

Would the people who live with you or work with you secretly say that you harbor some bitterness?

Look at the following passage with me and answer the question that follows the Scripture:

Make sure no man, woman, family group, or tribe among you leaves the Lord our God to go and serve the gods of those nations. They would be to you like a plant that grows bitter, poisonous fruit. **Deuteronomy 29:18,** NCV

What choice does this passage warn against?

What happens to the person who leaves God?

How can turning away from God in your life begin to cause a bitterness?

I have decided that some people actually want you to become bitter. They encourage your resentment and feed your self-pity and indignation. They want you to be angry and get revenge. Doom-and-gloom scenarios become the most prominent topics of conversation. They've given in to bitter, and they want you to be bitter too. Bitterness is not self-contained. It's an infectious disease that harms everyone who comes in contact with it. Then when we're all infected, we can be in the bitter club together and compare bitter notes over dinner.

Do any people in your life encourage you to remain bitter instead of growing through your trials? Why do you suppose bitterness loves company?

Are you one of those people who discourages others? Sometimes that discouragement sounds something like this:

"I'd still be mad if I were you."
"I don't know why you just let that go."
"You should get revenge."

We get some weird satisfaction in revisiting our bitter memories. Reminding ourselves of the ones who have hurt us. Revisiting every time we have been treated unfairly or unjustly. Planning how to get even. Sulking. Brooding. Remembering.

I have certainly been a baby girl all by myself, without any assistance or prodding from anyone. When life catches you off guard, it's so easy to give in to bitterness, wallow in the failure and brokenness. I too have whined, cried, and pouted at life. I have been hurt and rejected. I have been misrepresented and unheard. I'm embarrassed to tell you how easily I've given up some days. I have tasted the root of bitterness, but I have come to regard its comfort as poison.

I do not want to become a bitter old woman. I do not want to remain inward, focused on my grievances. We cannot stay that way and go forward with God. More than anything else, I want to be a grown-up woman. I want to become a mature follower of my Lord Jesus Christ.

> I do not want to remain inward, focused on my grievances. We cannot stay that way and go forward with God.

How does bitterness stunt our spiritual and emotional growth?

We all certainly have bitter old woman potential. Give that some thought for a minute. What would living in bitterness do to your future? Your family? Your heart?

The mature woman in Christ feels pain. She suffers great life disappointments. She knows rejection, loss, and loneliness. She could give you a hundred reasons why life hasn't turned out or why every day could be awful. But the mature follower resists living in bitterness. She doesn't surrender to this desperate attitude because in her grown-up faith she has learned to believe God instead.

This week, the question for your heart is: Will you resist bitterness and choose instead to believe God more?

When the circumstances are dark—believe God.
When the way is unclear—believe God.
When no one is for you—believe God.
When all hope is lost—believe God.

What uncertainty or pain do you face today? Write it below, and then in bold letters write a reminder to yourself—BELIEVE GOD!

You may have a hundred reasons calling you toward bitterness, but believing God—no matter what—is the conviction that will lead you out.

Day 2

Choosing to Believe

Daily Prayer Praise

"For I know the plans I have for you," declares the LORD, *"plans to prosper you and not to harm you, plans to give you hope and a future."*

Jeremiah 29:11

I made a new friend a few years ago, a lanky mid-fifties guy with a very intense, very secular 80-hour-a-week career. Divorced, for 10 years he has lived alone, trying to co-parent with someone who is difficult to deal with. His children are angry with their mother, and they've given him plenty of heartache. But the day I met this man, he came through the door happy. I'm not kidding, he was genuinely happy.

This very unassuming, ordinary-to-look-at man stands apart in character and countenance. So happy, in fact, that his presence lights up every room we've ever been in. Not only that, we're now three years into meetings and programs, and his spirit has been consistently and remarkably the same in every encounter we've ever had. Peaceful and positive and looking for good, he's fun to be with. All his colleagues hold him in high esteem. He is respected in his profession and regarded as wise and insightful. The man is not bitter, but he's just like us, he's got a hundred reasons he could be.

One day I took him to lunch to ask the burning questions, "Where in the world did your countenance come from? Are you always happy?"

"Angela, do you think I have a happy-go-lucky, carefree life without any sadness?"

"No, I realize that your life circumstances have been difficult, that's why I'm so interested in hearing about your heart and your thinking. I have rarely met someone like you. Your spirit is full. You radiate a light that touches everyone you meet. Tell me what it is."

"I believe God."

"Somehow, I knew you were going to say that."

Do you embody Ephesians 4:30-32? If not, what is a small step you can take to work towards that?

Do not grieve the Holy Spirit of God, by whom you were sealed for the day of redemption.

Let all bitterness and wrath and anger and clamor and slander be put away from you, along with all malice.

Be kind to one another, tender-hearted, forgiving each other, just as God in Christ also has forgiven you.

Ephesians 4:30-32

Every time I have allowed myself to fall into bitterness and disappointment, I realize that it's because I have listened to Satan's prompting. I have inclined my head toward his directives. I have forgotten to live what I believe. I have forgotten that my God is on the throne of all creation. God's heart toward me is good. His promises are true. His Son is my Savior.

This seems like the perfect place to stop and remember the promises of God. Look up as many of these truths as you have time for. Come back if you want on another day. Tape a new promise over your kitchen sink. Remember God. Remember what you believe.

God promises ...

... that nothing is too hard for Him.	**Genesis 18:12-14**
... to fight for you.	**Exodus 14:14**
... to remember His promise.	**Deuteronomy 4:31**
... to watch you constantly.	**2 Chronicles 16:9**
... you will never be in need.	**Psalm 23:1**
... that His purposes never change.	**Psalm 33:11**
... never to desert you.	**Psalm 37:28**
... to rescue you from the power of death.	**Psalm 49:15**
... to be faithful.	**Psalm 71:22**
... to command His angels to protect you.	**Psalm 91:11**
... that everything He has planned will happen.	**Isaiah 14:24**
... to love you forever.	**Isaiah 55:3**
... to give you a new heart.	**Ezekiel 36:26**
... to be your King.	**Micah 2:13**
... to strengthen you.	**Zechariah 10:12**
... you will have rest.	**Matthew 11:28**
... anything can be forgiven.	**Mark 3:28**
... freedom.	**Luke 4:18**
... blessing.	**John 1:16**

... to be your friend.	**John 15:14-15**
... to save you.	**Acts 2:21**
... comfort.	**2 Corinthians 1:3-4**
... you are His child by faith.	**Galatians 3:26**
... to have a plan for you.	**Ephesians 2:10**
... courage and confidence.	**Ephesians 3:12**
... to complete a good work in you.	**Philippians 1:6**
... to relieve you from your troubles.	**2 Thessalonians 1:7-8**
... to help when you are tempted.	**Hebrews 2:18**
... a share in His kingdom to you.	**James 2:5**
... to honor humble people.	**James 4:6,10**
... to listen to you.	**1 Peter 3:12**
... to defend you.	**1 John 2:1**
... eternal life.	**1 John 2:25**
... to come soon.	**Revelation 22:20**

Maybe you have forgotten to believe God sometimes too.

Maybe you have every earthly right to feel bitter and resentful, but it's been long enough now. It's time to let go of this sickly method of coping. You desire the way out. You want to dance with God toward His plans and His purpose. You want to know a genuine happiness that circumstances cannot stain.

Which of God's promises do you need to recommit to believing?

One more thing. Does someone you love need to be reminded to believe too? Choose the promise above. Look up the passage in your favorite translation, and then before you forget, just text the verse to your friend. You non-texters will have to write a note and put it in the mail. But either way, don't forget. God wants you to give away the encouragement you have been given!

If you are tired of bitterness and the despair that it brings, then pay close attention to the next three days on choosing. They could very well help you be free of bitterness. Not just a little free. You could be finally and fully free.

Day 3

Choose Freedom

Daily Prayer Praise

The Spirit of the Sovereign LORD *is on me, because the* LORD *has anointed me to preach good news to the poor. He has sent me to bind up the brokenhearted, to proclaim freedom for the captives and release from darkness for the prisoners.*

Isaiah 61:1

Some might look at the woman finding comfort in bitterness and shake their heads. "She'll probably never be free," they might whisper.

Many think no easy steps to freedom exist. Becoming free is a process that takes a long time, maybe even a lifetime. Only after a lot of hard work and years of failing, could you choose to believe in the power of God and learn to stay in His freedom.

But it doesn't have to be that way. I think you can choose to believe God today and that choosing will radically and powerfully begin to change every aspect of the way you interact with life and the people you love. I have seen the power of God to change hearts instantly, and so I am going out on a limb here.

You can choose to begin believing God **today** *and actually stay there no matter what comes to you.*

So, today let's choose freedom from our bitterness. Here's how I think we should begin. I'm sure you've seen similar cleansing steps before, but they bear repeating in this context.

Steps to Releasing Bitterness

1. Confess any tendency you have toward bitterness. Maybe your nature has always been to be bitter. Maybe you learned bitterness in your upbringing. Even a lifetime of patterns does not have to own your future. Our God is more than able to change your nature and your learned habits. If you aren't sure if you harbor bitterness, just ask someone who lives or works with you. They probably have a pretty clear picture of what you cannot see.

Praying prayers of confession is difficult for many of us, but just come in humility, knowing that God is truly in love with you. Ask Him to remove every root of bitterness and all tendencies to grow more such roots.

2. Receive God's cleansing forgiveness. Remember, forgiveness is for forgiveness. Forgiveness should make us grateful.

Really, truly, take some moments in prayer and quiet to receive this gift from God.

3. Relinquish the old desire to harbor bitterness. Some people call this surrender, a spiritual giving up. It feels like an emotional deep breath to me where I picture anger and resentment being drained from my body and being filled instead with the fresh, life-giving breath of God. I realize that may sound a little hokey to you, but giving up the practice of bitterness is a conscious act of your will. Paul said, "Get rid of all bitterness" (Eph. 4:31). It is difficult for us, but God gives us the power to do what He has asked us to do.

> I picture the anger and resentment being drained from my body and being filled instead with the fresh, life-giving breath of God.

4. Reject Satan's lies. Satan continues to deceive. He whispers that you will find comfort in bitterness.

5. Apply God's grace to the people and circumstances in your life. I've had women tell me this feels nearly impossible to them. I hear you. But this is where you take a step of maturity by faith or you remain locked inside the bitter jail. Forgiving as you have been forgiven. Choosing to lay aside your judgment. Trusting God for your future and for His better. Allowing others to prosper. Waiting for God. Each act of maturity requires grace. God will give every grace you need to grow.

6. Believe God. Here's what I know to be true. God really does have a plan, a purpose, and a future for each of us. He is sovereign and fully in control. He provides a way out and a way up. He redeems suffering and disciplines us from His Father-heart. He still loves broken people, and He mends their brokenness.

We have a certain hope because we belong to God. Believing in that hope no matter what can wipe away every inclination we have toward bitterness. Halfhearted believing keeps us tripping along through the faith. Lean in. Put all your weight on the promises of God. Live the Bible without reservation and watch the God of your hope show up.

See to it that no one misses the grace of God and that no bitter root grows up to cause trouble and defile many.
Hebrews 12:15

7. Start over at confession every time you need to until bitterness has no hold. Being human is frustrating. I want to choose and then have it done forever. But my humanity keeps me on my knees asking again and again to be free. My imperfection keeps me fully dependent on the grace of God. For me, staying free means staying in the presence of God. And in the presence of God, bitterness will lose its attraction. The taste of it will eventually become repulsive and childish to you.

Bitterness keeps you shackled to the wall of immaturity, but Jesus Christ has made a way for you to be set free. He has shown us how to set our minds above and pursue a life that imitates Him. The key to freedom has been given to you by grace.

So today, reach down and pick up the key. The lock that keeps you in prison is on the inside. Today, by the grace of God, you can let yourself out.

Write a prayer expressing your heart to God about freedom from bitterness.

God does not waste suffering, nor does He discipline out of caprice. If He plow, it is because He purposes a crop.
J. Oswald Sanders [2]

Day 4

Choose Wisdom

Through the years, I have often prayed and asked God to make me wise. I don't think I realized what a big deal this was going to be or how much wisdom comes to us through pain and discipline. God lays before us the path of wisdom, but we have to choose it for ourselves. Foolishness comes easily and is often the natural consequence of not choosing wisely.

Wisdom is a gift that God gives to the woman who pursues it. Have you asked God to make you wise?
☐ yes ☐ no

Name three of the wisest people you know:

1.

2.

3.

How do you believe someone becomes wise?

If you had to make a plan to go after wisdom, how would your plan begin?

To God belong wisdom and power; counsel and understanding are his.

Job 12:13

What would motivate you to pursue greater wisdom?

*Wisdom is supreme;
therefore get wisdom.
Though it cost all you
have, get understanding.*
Proverbs 4:7

Every morning during the school year, my clock goes off at 5:45 a.m. I have had a child in school for 13 years, and I'm still not over having to wake up so early. Almost every day I lie there for the eight snooze minutes and tell myself, *You have to be the grown-up. No one is going to get the children up and ready for school unless you do it. Get up, Angela. Be a big girl. Come on.*

Getting everybody up, fed, and off to school is my responsibility. It goes along with being a parent and a grown-up. But I still have to tell myself to do it. I still have to choose every morning to be responsible and mature. I believe it's much the same way with wisdom.

Wisdom can be just down the hall waiting for us, but we can lie in the bed and keep hitting the snooze when calls us awake. It's just easier not to kick off the covers of our foolishness. It takes effort to throw our feet over the side of the bed and make our way toward right living. Choosing wisdom means that you are deciding to be a big girl and act like a big girl even when the little girl inside you wants to stay in bed.

It's the foolish little girl inside of us who wants to hold on to bitterness. The whole book of Proverbs teaches us over and over—choose wisdom and you will receive blessing, choose foolishness and suffer the consequences.

Look at this wisdom passage with me:

A Girlfriend Nudge

Read the whole Book of Proverbs and underline everything the book says about fools. Wisdom means removing foolishness from your life. Do a heart and life check to keep yourself from foolishness.

> *My child, hold on to wisdom and good sense.*
>   *Don't let them out of your sight.*
> **They will give you life**
>   **and beauty like a necklace around your neck.**
> *Then you will go your way in safety,*
>   *and you will not get hurt.*
> *When you lie down, you won't be afraid;*
>   *when you lie down, you will sleep in peace.*
> *You won't be afraid of sudden trouble;*
>   *you won't fear the ruin that comes to the wicked,*
> *because the Lord will keep you safe.*
>   *He will keep you from being trapped.*
> **Proverbs 3:21-26, NCV, emphasis mine**

As you begin to resist bitterness and choose wisdom, God promises His blessing and protection.

I've met plenty of grown-up women who have lived their whole lives bitter and resentful. Not one of them would ever be regarded as wise. Childish? Yes. Immature? You betcha. Wise woman of God? No way.

In the Bible, the apostle Paul says,

> *When I was a child, I talked like a child, I thought like a child, I reasoned like a child. When I became a man, I stopped those childish ways.*
> **1 Corinthians 13:11, NCV**

Confident women believe in God. They choose wisdom and resist the childish ways of bitterness.

Choosing wisdom often means making an everyday exchange in life. It means that you decide to choose differently, respond differently, or pursue different ideas or relationships. For instance, the woman who wants a healthier body will have to choose wisdom. Then maybe wisdom would tell her to pass on the sticky bun for breakfast.

We all know becoming a godly woman and growing up in our salvation means facing much bigger choices than sticky buns. Sometimes there is so much. But today, where could you begin?

Consider the following areas of your life, and consider whether or not wisdom would ask you to choose differently.

Your physical body:

Your family:

Your work or career:

Your friendships:

Your social life:

Your private life:

Your spiritual life:

Now take a look at some of the blessings that come from wisdom. Underline all the instructions to get wisdom. Circle all the blessings.

> When I was a boy at my father's knee,
>   the pride and joy of my mother,
> He would sit me down and drill me:
>   "Take this to heart. Do what I tell you—live!
> Sell everything and buy Wisdom! Forage for Understanding!
>   Don't forget one word! Don't deviate an inch!
> Never walk away from Wisdom—she guards your life;
>   love her—she keeps her eye on you.
> Above all and before all, do this: Get Wisdom!
>   Write this at the top of your list: Get Understanding!
> Throw your arms around her—believe me, you won't regret it;
>   never let her go—she'll make your life glorious.
> She'll garland your life with grace,
>   she'll festoon your days with beauty."
> **Proverbs 4:3-9, MSG**

Spiritual maturity walks hand in hand with the woman who seeks to be wise in the Lord.

Before we end, decide to choose wisdom and pray for wisdom. Believe me, spiritual maturity walks hand in hand with the woman who seeks to be wise in the Lord.

Day 5

Choose Victory

Do you remember the story about a woman who came to church for the very first time in her life? She heard the truth about Jesus that day and came to the front of the church to meet with the pastor. They talked for a while and the woman decided to trust Jesus as her Savior. The pastor wanted to meet with the woman in a week but told her she should get a Bible and begin reading.

The next day the brand-new believer came running into the pastor's office. "Preacher, I bought a Bible like you said, and I've been reading it all day. I couldn't wait a week. I just had to come talk to you."

Curious about what was so urgent, the pastor asked, "What did you read?"

"Well, I didn't know where to begin, so when it flipped open to the Book of Revelation I started there."

The pastor felt a little uneasy. This woman who had never been to church in her life began reading the Bible in one of the most difficult books to understand. "What did you learn?" the pastor hesitantly inquired.

"We win!" the woman exclaimed. "At the end, we win!"

The pastor smiled at the woman's understanding, "You're exactly right. We do win."

Maybe it hasn't been at the forefront of your thoughts lately, but we do win. The victory belongs to God. Evil will be punished. Righteousness will be rewarded. Every knee will bow before the King of heaven and earth. This train really is bound for glory.

How does remembering the truth of our victory make you feel?

Daily Prayer Praise

Conquerors will march in the victory parade, their names indelible in the Book of Life. I'll lead them up and present them by name to my Father and his Angels.

Revelation 3:5, MSG

Do you know someone else who needs to be reminded today that we belong to God and the victory has already been won?
☐ yes ☐ no **If so, who? Write their initials here.** _____

You can choose this day to live in light of the victory that is promised. When a woman begins to live in the assurance of certain victory, holding on to bitterness loses its power. Bitterness fades in the bright light of celebration. As children of the Most High God, we have much to celebrate.

One day every tear will be wiped away. You will understand the purpose for every trial you have faced and the suffering you have known.

- You will no longer see through the mirror dimly **(1 Cor. 13:12).**
- Satan is doomed. Evil will be bound and punished for eternity **(Rev. 20:2).**
- You will enter into the promise of a new heaven and a new earth forever **(Isa. 65:17).**
- You will finally be as God has always dreamed you would be.
- Victory belongs to every one who calls Jesus Lord **(1 John 2:14).**

Read what John wrote to us:

God's commands are not too hard for us, because everyone who is a child of God conquers the world. And this is the victory that conquers the world—our faith. So the one who conquers the world is the person who believes that Jesus is the Son of God.
1 John 5:3-5, NCV

How would things begin to change in your life if you began choosing to live in the victory that's already certain?

I think that if we believed God and kept heaven in view, much that invites us to bitterness would fall away.

- You would not have to vie for position. Your place with God is certain.
- You could lay aside your judgment. God is the final judge.

☐ You could look forward to new adventure instead of back at every failure.
☐ Getting even would mean nothing. Getting right with God would mean everything.

Try to think of three ways you could begin to live in the truth of God's victory:

1.

2.

3.

In view of eternity and the victory that is sure, we can choose to become grown-up Jesus women. We can hear the Holy Spirit call and choose to get up and face our battles with courage instead of a bitter heart.

A few weeks ago I was teaching at a women's conference. It wasn't a part of what I'd planned to say, but for some reason I went down this path:

> *I am a single mom. I have four kids that I provide for. I am not dating. There is no one to catch me except Jesus. Life hasn't really turned out right, but Jesus is my Lord and I am not bitter.*

The women burst into applause and began to stand. Their enthusiasm shocked me at first. They were cheering the decision to believe God instead of living bitter. Maybe it would help if you knew all of heaven did the same. Every time you believe God and resist bitterness, I'm sure the angels stand to applaud.

And every time you resist bitterness, that keeps God from having to stop the car, pull you over to the side of the road, and give you the *look-at-your-life-and-be-grateful-for-the-crackers-you-have* sermon.

Every time you believe God and resist bitterness, I'm sure the angels stand to applaud.

Pray out loud the words of 1 Corinthians 15:57: "Thanks be to God, who gives us the victory through our Lord Jesus Christ!"

Then write a prayer thanking God for victory.

---

1. Stephen Brown, *When Your Rope Breaks* (Nashville: Thomas Nelson, 1988), 79.

2. J. Oswald Sanders, introduction to *Green Leaf in Drought-time,* by Isobel Kuhn (Chicago: Moody, 1957), 7.

Prayer

Oh Father,

I recognize my own weakness. I see the potential inside of me. Except for Your grace, I could become hard and bitter toward this world.

Lord, keep me soft and tender in heart. Help me see like You see. Let me feel the way You feel. Turn my attention away from myself and let me focus on giving away what You have already given to me.

Let me give forgiveness. Let me give mercy. Let me give joy. Make me a radiant woman. A woman who dances in Your arms. A woman who is wrapped in Your glory. A woman who is learning to lay down her very life so that You might be glorified in mine.

I love You, sweet Jesus.

Amen

Sometimes the wallflower has to get ready, get to the ballroom, and then patiently wait for her turn to dance.

Until It's Your Turn

Week 5

Day 1

Not Yet

Life can sometimes be like standing in line. You get all your stuff together. Pack a snack. Choose the appropriate path. Muster up your patience. Square your determination. And wait to be next.

A great lesson comes to those who spend the good part of a lifetime waiting on different things. Sometimes you have all your papers and the necessary credentials, you are in exactly the right line at exactly the right time, but you still have to wait. An agonizing wait. An I-wonder-if-I'm-in-the-right-line wait. A much longer wait than you had expected. All the time, you may be in the right place, facing the right direction, but maybe it's just not your turn yet.

Are there areas of your life where you believe it's just not your turn? If so, what are those areas?

The mature woman knows how to wait on God. She has learned through tears, disappointment, and even rejection that some-times it's just not your turn. That doesn't mean that it won't ever be. Or that you're not qualified. Or that you've gone completely the wrong way. It's just not yet. John Piper wrote:

> We are like farmers. They plow the field and plant the seed and cut away weeds and scare away crows, but they do not make the crop grow. God does. He sends rain and sunshine and brings to maturity the hidden life of the seed. We have our part. But it is not coercive or controlling. And there will be times when the crops fail. Even then God has his ways of feeding the farmer and bringing him through a lean season. We must learn to wait for the Lord. [1]

To do everything we can, stay the course, and wait to be next requires a grown-up Jesus woman who has put away whining and manipulation. She has decided not to stomp her feet, huff and puff, groan and complain. She is waiting with integrity. Not

Daily Prayer Praise

*We wait in hope for
  the LORD;
  he is our help and
  our shield.
In him our hearts rejoice,
  for we trust in his
  holy name.*

Psalm 33:20-21

cutting in line with her friend who's further ahead. Not cheating for advantage. Not bargaining or bribing. Just waiting until her time comes and she is called.

Read the following Scriptures and underline the word *waiting* or *wait* in each one. Put a star next to the ones that speak to you and your current situations.

In the morning, O LORD, you hear my voice; in the morning I lay my requests before you and wait in expectation.
Psalm 5:3

Be still before the LORD and wait patiently for him; do not fret when men succeed in their ways, when they carry out their wicked schemes.
Psalm 37:7

Yes, LORD, walking in the way of your laws, we wait for you; your name and renown are the desire of our hearts.
Isaiah 26:8

But if we hope for what we do not yet have, we wait for it patiently.
Romans 8:25

And so after waiting patiently, Abraham received what was promised.
Hebrews 6:15

So Christ was sacrificed once to take away the sins of many people; and he will appear a second time, not to bear sin, but to bring salvation to those who are waiting for him.
Hebrews 9:28

Which verse speaks most to the kind of waiting you are currently having to deal with, and why?

This lesson of *Not Yet* may be the one that most profoundly shapes my character and my heart. You really have to trust God to wait. You must believe in His divine love. You must lean into His arms and stop fidgeting with your own agenda. You must surrender your five-year plan and give up your pride. Waiting requires so much maturity that I understand why most of us just get out of line, abandoning what we've been made for because the wait seemed too long.

Almost every arena of life requires a wait that is beyond my own ability. My professional career demands that I wait for approval. It mandates a public testing that will confirm or refute my readiness to go forward. The Lord beckons me to keep my eyes on Him, continue to walk in my calling, and understand that sometimes it's just not my turn.

My mothering waits for fruit. Will all these years sow character in the ones that I love? I see glimpses. I hope for more. Holding my breath. Praying my guts out. Waiting for the seeds and planting and pruning to grow into godly, faithful lives.

My heart waits to be loved by a man. It is an almost unceasing ache too painful to describe. Night after night of lonely integrity. Week after week of being a single mom in a family church. Another Valentine's Day bouquet from my sweet dad. Going on. Making plans. Buying a house. Putting up the Christmas tree. Alone. Trusting God. Waiting for my turn.

In each place I hear the Holy Spirit whisper, *Stay in line. Do not rush ahead of God. Stand with your head up. Stand with honor. Soon, it will be your turn.*

Oh my goodness, life requires us to wait. Some of my close friends wait for an adoption agency in China to tell them they can come for their daughter. Another friend waits for a degree she wishes she'd gotten 20 years ago. My high-school girlfriend is waiting for 10 more chemo treatments, a double mastectomy, and radiation to be completed. As this mother of two waits for restored health, each of her days is graciously teaching the rest of us about courage and complete dependence.

Let's return to the altar we talked about in week 1. Do you remember the altar where you knelt and laid your heart before the Lord? Do you remember how it felt to lay everything in truth before the only One who can help? Let's return to the Lord today with the truth of our waiting.

Remember every little and big thing you wait for.

Now lay all those things on the altar of your faithful God.

And pray a prayer of commitment.

Tell God you will keep waiting on Him.

> *Wait on God and He will work, but don't wait in spiritual sulks because you cannot see an inch in front of you!*
> **—Oswald Chambers** [2]

It's OK to be weak. Tell the Lord. It's OK to be tired and cry out from your weariness. Just go to your altar and lay down all that you wait for. I am trusting that God will meet you there.

Day 2

Abide

Daily Prayer Praise

Great are the works of
*   the LORD;*
*   they are pondered by*
*   all who delight in*
*   them.*
Glorious and majestic
*   are his deeds,*
*   and his righteousness*
*   endures forever.*
He has caused his
*   wonders to be*
*   remembered;*
*   the LORD is gracious*
*   and compassionate*

Psalm 111:2-4

So how then shall we wait? If spiritual maturity is our goal and the fullness of the Holy Spirit is our desire, then how shall we wait before God? Waiting is not whining or fretting or looking over to compare whose turn came before ours. Waiting is an opportunity to grow up. To wait upon the Lord means choosing a higher road that most are not willing to take. Sometimes the wallflower has to wait to dance.

> **How does reframing your wait from something to endure to a God-given invitation to maturity change your attitude about the situation?**

The big baby inside of me is about three years old, and she wants to stomp her feet and scream for attention. She doesn't want to wait her turn. She wants to rush ahead to the front. She wants all the people who've ever pushed her aside to be pushed back. And she desperately wants to pout. When one of my kids would pout, I would turn my head and smile, but when I meet a grown-up woman who pouts, I want to turn my head and roll my eyes.

God help us all from giving in to the baby girl. It's time to put away her childish behavior. Until it's your turn, which by the way, seems to come so much more slowly for the whiners, there is an opportunity to choose the better way of maturity and spiritual growth. A long time ago I heard the adage, "You haven't begun to wait until you think you've waited long enough." By the time we're 35, most of us feel like we could write "Enough waiting already" across all the pages in our journals. But maybe it's not about the length of time you have been waiting. Maybe what matters more is how.

How would you describe the way you have waited on God?

God gives us many desires that require a determined wait. The longing for romantic love. The desire to improve and use our gifts. A home that becomes a haven for family and friends. A strong physical body. The blessing of children. But the journey of desire is not a rocket ride. It's a spiritual marathon and maybe even more than the desire itself, what matters is how you run toward it.

So how shall we wait? What are we supposed to do until it's our turn? The following principles can help us wait in strength for our desires. As you take inventory of your waiting, whether spiritual, emotional, or physical, decide that you will make adjustments where necessary. Determine that you'll do whatever it takes to implement these directives. Sometimes it's just not your turn, but God wants to do amazing things in your life in the meantime.

Principles for Waiting

And so, the very first thing I believe God asks of the person who is waiting their turn is:

1. Abide. Until it's your turn, God is asking you to stay with Him. Don't go anywhere. Remain. Stay. He wants you in His presence, moment by moment, so that step-by-step you hear His voice and turn at His will. Here's where most of us give up. The wait feels too long, so we assume God doesn't care. We push away from His presence to hurry things up.

In John 15, Jesus gave the Upper Room instructions to His disciples. Read verses 1-10 in the margin and circle the word *remain* every time Jesus uses it.

"I am the true vine, and my Father is the gardener. He cuts off every branch in me that bears no fruit, while every branch that does bear fruit he prunes so that it will be even more fruitful. ... Remain in me, and I will remain in you. No branch can bear fruit by itself; it must remain in the vine. Neither can you bear fruit unless you remain in me. I am the vine; you are the branches. If a man remains in me and I in him, he will bear much fruit; apart from me you can do nothing. If anyone does not remain in me, he is like a branch that is thrown away and withers ... If you remain in me and my words remain in you, ask whatever you wish, and it will be given you. This is to my Father's glory, that you bear much fruit, showing yourselves to be my disciples. ... Now remain in my love. If you obey my commands, you will remain in my love, just as I have obeyed my Father's commands and remain in his love."
John 15:1-10

Remain in me.
—Jesus, John 15:4

A Girlfriend Nudge

What if you extend your prayer time for the next few days? These nudges are supposed to be for spiritual stretching. So, how about spending 30 minutes in uninterrupted prayer for three days in a row? Just a nudge to help you grow!

On this evening before His betrayal and arrest, He told His followers that in the coming days they would need to remain with Him. Abide. Stay put. Wait. He was so concerned that they understand the importance of abiding that in 10 verses He told them 11 times to *remain*. Those instructions continue with great relevance for our lives. While you are waiting—as you go, in season and out of season—you are called to remain with God.

I love the writings of Andrew Murray. He knew so very much about the grace of God. For those of us who view abiding as another thing we have to figure out how to do, he wrote:

> Abiding in Christ is just meant for the weak, and so beautifully suited to their feebleness. It is not the doing of some great thing, and does not demand that we first lead a very holy and devoted life. No, it is simply weakness entrusting itself to a Mighty One to be kept,—the unfaithful one casting self on One who is altogether trustworthy and true. Abiding in Him is not a work that we have to do as the condition for enjoying His salvation, but a consenting to let Him do all for us, and in us, and through us. It is a work He does for us. [3]

Arriving at our destination gives us new energy. We feel a surge of enthusiasm and resolve to push across the finish line. Enough spiritual adrenaline to keep going.

But waiting. Waiting is so draining. We begin to stumble, lose focus, and doubt. I love that the abiding Murray writes about is "for the weak." A tired woman like you or me. We can do that. We can lean in and ask God to take hold of us. To abide is to consent in your mind and in your spirit to give yourself to God for His keeping. Here is where you can be assured that the wallflower can fall into the strong arms of God and agree to stay there. He is the One who will lift you up to dance at exactly the right time.

~~~~~~

As we conclude this day, give God your promise to stay in His arms.

Entrust and Trust

If I had something valuable that needed to be kept safe, let's say an antique vase, there's no way I'd entrust it to one of my children. They might intend to take care of it, but before you knew it, that heirloom would be full of kid treasures like gel pens and sticky candy, complete with glow-in-the-dark slime at the bottom. Nope, if I wanted my vase taken care of, I'd give it to my friend Lisa. The next time I needed it, I'm sure she'd know exactly where it was, right in the bin labeled *Keep for Angela,* bubble-wrapped, and packed into a sturdy crate. I can be sure that anything I entrust to Lisa will come back better than I gave it to her. She's just that kind of organized, thoughtful, meticulous friend.

Think back to our list of things God wants us to do while we wait. We started yesterday with abide. Consider the next element of effective waiting.

2. Entrust. I believe that the second thing God calls us to do while we wait is the conscious act of entrusting. We entrust to God what we regard as valuable.

If Lisa would be careful with my vase, can you imagine how much more vigilant God will be with your heart's desire? He is both the Creator and Master Planner. He is the Giver of your desires. You are a dreaming and becoming woman because you have been made that way. You are full of life and full of the desire for more life. You can entrust to God your heart, every need, and every longing. As a matter of fact, you can begin to trust Him so much that your waiting becomes a beautiful offering. An act of devotion. A sacrifice of praise.

What do you regard as valuable in this season of your life?

Daily Prayer Praise

Yet I am not ashamed, because I know whom I have believed, and am convinced that he is able to guard what I have entrusted to him for that day.

2 Timothy 1:12

Not many months ago I was speaking to a large group of women at a retreat center. Between the sessions I met privately with several women for conversation or prayer. That weekend, one particular struggle just kept coming up. Several of the women, all unknown to each other, were involved in extramarital affairs or were actively considering having an affair. I always assume that one brave woman speaks for about 10 others and so the weight of each new confession left me increasingly sad and heavyhearted.

During the last teaching session, as God would have it, I was speaking to the women about entrusting their hearts and dreams to Jesus. His great love. His capable hands. His understanding heart.

On that day I felt I should share my own longings. I told them something like this:

You all know that I am a single mom. I'm 41. Some say that I'm in the prime of my life and I'd have to agree. These years are very beautiful and exciting to me. But they are not without sadness or disappointment. There is a painful loneliness that can come to the feminine soul. We were made for romantic, intimate love and without it, the heart becomes weary and longing begins to magnify the emptiness.

I am not dating. I also don't have any sense that dating or marriage is in my near future. But I am a woman, and I have all the same desires that come with being made feminine. So some days and nights my longing becomes grieving.

Some well-meaning people have said to me, "God will be your husband." To which I wanted to reply, "You're a nerd," but I haven't. I realize people mean well and they want to give comfort, but they don't have words for what they haven't experienced or the emptiness they've long forgotten.

Here's what I know. God made me for the arms of a man. His design. His idea. He is very aware that my heart longs for romance and physical intimacy. He also knows that my prime years are skipping right by. Here is what I have said to God:

Father, I entrust to You my sexuality. I give You my heart of desire. I lay all my romantic dreams at Your feet. Paris in the fall, tropical island getaways. I speak to You in honesty and in righteousness. It's just me. The woman You made. Entrusting my longings to the God I love. Would You keep all the treasures of my heart safe until Your appointed time? Would You return to me, with multiplied joy, all the years that I wait? And God, if it would be OK with You, I'd like to have sex with a loving husband before menopause.

Are you willing to entrust whatever is precious or desired to your Father who has promised to be faithful?

The psalmist said:

> *People, trust God all the time. Tell him all your problems, because God is our protection.*
> **Psalm 62:8, NCV**

I am believing with my whole life that while we wait, God can be entrusted to protect and defend the treasures of the woman He loves. I also believe that entrusting is an act of submission. To submit to God as Lord. To entrust and believe in His love with your treasure.

> God can be entrusted to protect and defend the treasures of the woman He loves.

3. Trust. We entrust our treasure for safekeeping and then we are called to trust the One to whom they have been given. I believe Brennan Manning explained trusting God best in this passage from his book, *Ruthless Trust*:

> When the brilliant ethicist John Kavanaugh went to work for three months at "the house of the dying" in Calcutta, he was seeking a clear answer as to how best to spend the rest of his life. On the first morning there he met Mother Teresa. She asked, "And what can I do for you?" Kavanaugh asked her to pray for him.
> "What do you want me to pray for?" she asked. He voiced the request that he had borne thousands of miles from the United States: "Pray that I have clarity."
> She said firmly, "No, I will not do that." When he asked her why, she said, "Clarity is the last thing you are clinging to and must let go of." When Kavanaugh commented that *she* always seemed to have the clarity he longed for, she laughed and said, "I have never had clarity; what I have always had is trust. So I will pray that you trust God."
> "We ourselves have known and put our trust in God's love toward ourselves" (1 John 4:16). Craving clarity, we attempt to eliminate the risk of trusting God. Fear of the unknown path stretching ahead of us destroys childlike trust in the Father's active goodness and unrestricted love.

We often presume that trust will dispel the confusion, illuminate the darkness, vanquish the uncertainty, and redeem the times. But the crowd of witnesses in Hebrews 11 testifies that this is not the case. Our trust does not bring final clarity on this earth. It does not still the chaos or dull the pain or provide a crutch. When all else is unclear, the heart of trust says, as Jesus did on the cross, "Into your hands I commit my spirit." (Luke 23:46) [4]

And so, will you entrust your treasure to God and then trust that He is able to keep it safe until His timing is revealed?

Day 4

Become

Daily Prayer Praise

You are a shield around me, O LORD;
you bestow glory on me and lift up my head.

Psalm 3:3

I hope you've been thinking about trusting God more this week. We've seen our need to abide. We've challenged ourselves to entrust our greatest valuables to God and trust Him to care for them. Today let's move to the next step.

4. Become. When it's finally your turn, wouldn't it be devastating not to be ready? God would say, "Next." And you'd say, "Can I get a few more minutes? I'm not quite there yet." In this season of waiting, you and I are responsible for becoming ready, preparing to step up when we're called. Being shaped into the women God wants to use. The next step in our waiting is the personal decision to become the woman who is ready for God's call.

Have you thought much lately about who you are becoming?
☐ yes ☐ no

Describe the woman you have always wanted to be:

What have you always wanted to do?

What are three things you could begin doing for the purpose of becoming that woman?

1.

2.

3.

Sometimes after an event a woman will come to me and tell me she wants to do what I do. She would like to write books and speak to women. I always tell her to "Come on, there is so much work to be done. We need more women who are speaking and teaching and leading others toward the cross."

Then she'll graciously ask me for some pointers. Questions about how to get started or who to call or what to do. I almost hate those hopeful questions because I know that I'm getting ready to give her an answer she doesn't want to hear. She may have been hoping I'll give her a Web site or the name of an agent to call, but I only have a journey to share.

Twenty years ago, I knew that I wanted to do this too. I went to seminary to get ready. Then I went on staff at a church where my training with people began in earnest. For the next 15 years, I would teach anywhere anybody needed a woman like me to show up—the garden club, a last-minute replacement for the real speaker who missed her plane, or at some event where people are eating. For the record, it's very humbling to talk about anything—especially anything spiritual—while people are eating. They really don't care so much when there is food. I think all speakers should have to talk while food is being served a few times a year, just to maintain perspective.

So I've been doing the same thing, at this writing, for about 24 years. Using my stories to teach the Bible in fresh, energetic ways that women can apply to their lives. It's just that God has changed the venues in the past few years.

Is it possible that your becoming would require a journey?
☐ yes ☐ no

Could you commit to a journey to become the woman you have always wanted to be? ☐ yes ☐ no

Almost everywhere I go someone will say to me, "I had never heard of you before." I love that, because God has known me all along and all this time under His watchful care, I have been quietly becoming and waiting for my turn.

God knows you too. He crafted your gifts. He listens to your longings. He is interested in your dreams.

To this day I read everything I can get my hands on, listen to teaching CDs, and sleep with systematic theology books in stacks beside my bed. A total geek. Always learning. Still getting ready. Waiting for God to show me what's next.

While you wait, are you actively becoming the woman God can use? Are you faithful to prepare? I realize your life is busy, but when there is an hour or half a day, what do you do with it? I want to encourage you to make some life priorities and then spend any extra time you have focused on practical ways to become the woman you've dreamed of becoming.

What do you do instead of become? I am not talking about when you are exhausted or need rest. I mean when you have a little energy and a little time. Go to a movie? Walk through the mall? Sit in front of the television? I love entertainment, but I am so passionate about becoming that I try to be purposeful with my time. Reading work that feeds my mind. Listening to great speakers who shape my craft.

Make a quick list of the things you are inclined to choose instead of pursuing your becoming:

1.

2.

3.

4.

He works where He sends us to wait.
—Oswald Chambers [5]

A Girlfriend Nudge

Find a woman who is becoming in a way you desire to become. Buy her coffee. Ask her to tell you about the path she has taken. Just maybe, something she says could make the next step clear for you.

Now, look back and read what you wrote about the woman you want to become. Take all the distractions you wrote and exchange them with the pursuits God has put in your heart.

Don't delay. How many years have already gone by? Becoming is required in the waiting.

One day, you'll be next. If you're ready, it will be the thrill of a lifetime to step up for your turn in confidence. When God calls your name, you want to be ready to dance.

Day 5

Pray and Stand

For this journey we need to abide. We entrust and trust. We must prioritize what we desire to become. Today let's talk about what God wants us to become in our waits.

5. Pray. While you are waiting, God wants you to become and remain a woman of prayer.

Andrew Murray wrote:

> We must ... wait on God in prayer. [The disciples] waited, they prayed with one accord; prayer and supplication went up to God mingled with praise. They expected—our primary lesson—God in heaven to do something. I wish I could stress the importance of that! I find believers—and I have found in my own experience—who read, and understand, and think, and wish, and want to claim, and want to take, and want to get, and yet what they desire eludes their grasp. Why? Because they do not wait for God to give it. [6]

Prayer is the means by which we continually place ourselves into God's arms. When you meet a woman who is full of joy and confidence no matter what her circumstances, you have most likely encountered a woman of prayer.

Daily Prayer Praise

Before they call I will
answer;
while they are still
speaking I will hear.

Isaiah 65:24

How does prayer change your countenance?

I have the most vivid memories of a woman from my childhood church. Her countenance was genuinely peaceful. Her home was open and warm and inviting. Kids never felt the pressure to keep a lot of rules when we were with her, but that only made us want to please her more. After I was grown and had moved away, I came to know this childhood neighbor as a woman of prayer. That one characteristic made everything else about her make sense to me. Of course she prayed; everything we knew about her had been shaped by the years of consistent praying.

Prayer is the discipline by which God gives us the ability to wait. To persevere. To dream again. And to trust.

6. Stand. And after having done all these things, God may ask us to stand.

Two weeks ago my group of eight girlfriends met for a birthday lunch. We get together as often as possible, especially if gifts and food are involved. A local restaurant had a back room that we could pile into and amazingly, all of us were there. It almost seems statistically impossible, but each one of these women is a stay-at-home mom and very happily married. I am the only weird single mom in the bunch, and I'm very grateful they let me hang around.

What that means is that these friends have walked through a lot with me the past years. So much, in fact, that their arms should be tired of carrying me. This particular lunch was festive and fun. We hadn't all been together in too long. We had so much to catch up on. Just as everyone was about to leave, I had to totally bring the whole party down. I had been facing unrelenting attack in the past weeks and I was emotionally and spiritually exhausted. I felt God prompting me to ask for prayer. *These are your friends. Ask them to pray for you.* And so I did.

The minute they heard my voice quiver, these women moved from all around the table to touch me or hold me. *Single* means you don't get held much. I really needed to be held. Each one began to pray for and over me. My friend Jamie took my hands and said, "Angela, stand up."

Right in the middle of our back room at the Greek restaurant, decorated with party streamers and jumbled with little bags of gifts, I stood up, completely awash in tears. Sobbing. My girlfriends all stood around me. Then Jamie began to quote this passage and pray it for me:

> *Therefore put on the full armor of God, so that when the day of evil comes, you may be able to stand your ground, and **after you have done everything, to stand.***
> **Ephesians 6:13, emphasis mine**

Sometimes you have done everything you know to do. You abide in Christ and long for His presence. You entrust everything and everybody and keep entrusting day after day. You are faithful to become and change and to seek wisdom and growth. You pray. So that all that is left, after you have done everything, is to stand. Maybe you can't take one more step. Just stand. Maybe you're tired of the wait. Keep standing. Maybe it seems like it will never be your turn. Stand.

The physical act of standing up in that restaurant left me trembling. Jamie took hold of my hands with authority. She lovingly looked into my eyes. And then she instructed me, according to the admonition of Scripture, to stand. As an act of obedience to God, as a sign of my determined faith, there was nothing else to do except stand.

> Sometimes you have done everything you know to do. So all that is left is to stand.

In what areas of your life have you already done everything and realize that God is asking you to stand and wait?

Maybe today you don't know what else to do. You are tired and can't go forward. You have considered just getting out of line and abandoning the wait. Can I ask you to do something? If you are able in this moment, stand up. Physically stand up and pray:

> *God, I cannot see You. I have no idea what to do next. But as an act of my complete trust, I will stand. I will remain faithful and stay in my place until You show me what to do. Amen.*

Women face many conflicts. Lies we believe. Difficult relationships. Financial hardship. Whatever battle you face today, remember that it cannot have you. You belong to God. After you have done everything you can do, then stand and wait to see the glory of the Lord.

Wait on the Lord. Until it's your turn, I want you to become aware of God's intimate presence in your waiting. He is not far away. He is here. Holding you. I want you to know His pleasure. He is perfecting all those things that concern you.

God can give you a righteous confidence in your waiting. And when it's finally your turn and He says, "Next," what a thrill it will be to yell, "Hey, that's me! I'm ready to dance!"

1. John Piper, *When I Don't Desire God: How to Fight for Joy* (Wheaton, IL: Crossway Books, 2004), 42.

2. Oswald Chambers, *My Utmost for His Highest: The Classic Edition* (Uhrichsville, OH: Barbour, 1963), August 1.

3. Andrew Murray, *Abide in Christ: Thoughts on the Blessed Life of Fellowship with the Son of God* (New York: Grosset and Dunlap, n.d.), 24–25.

4. Brennan Manning, *Ruthless Trust: The Ragamuffin's Path to God* (San Francisco: Harper, 2000), 5–6.

5. Chambers, *My Utmost,* August 1.

6. Andrew Murrray, *The Believer's Absolute Surrender* (Minneapolis: Bethany House, 1985), 20.

Prayer

Lord Jesus,

Increase my patience. Renew my faithfulness. Teach me to trust. Let me learn how to wait with a righteous confidence.

Remind me that You have me and all that concerns me inside the safety of Your strong hands. Please remove my fears and the anxiousness I sometimes feel. Settle my heart where I have felt insecure. Help me to think clearly and boldly about the future You have planned for me. Lord, help me to trust. Trust you for the little and the big. For the earthly and the heavenly. Oh Lord, let me trust You fully.

And teach me how to rejoice even when I cannot see the answers or understand Your timing. Help me to do all that I can do and then patiently wait until You decide it's my turn.

With love and adoration,

Amen.

The wallflower, who never thought it possible, can be filled to the measure of all fullness by the amazing presence and power of the Holy Spirit. That fullness brings a righteous confidence and that's when wallflowers begin to dance.

The Spirit of God

Week 6

Day 1

The Power of the Holy Spirit

When I was a little girl, I was raised in a house of faith, but I did not understand salvation. Every night as I went to bed, I would beg God to take me to heaven if I died in my sleep. As I became older, I heard about "being saved," but it seemed extremist and outside my understanding of God. No one ever explained "being saved" to me, and I never pursued that foreign doctrine on my own. Still, I prayed every night and pleaded with God to save me from hell and allow me into heaven if I died while I slept. I'm not sure what I thought was going to happen if I kicked over during the day, but with the night my eternity always seemed more pressing.

Eventually, in college, I really came to understand the idea of being saved. As I began to understand this new information, what had once seemed outside what I had determined that I needed finally felt like exactly what I had been looking for all of my life. I prayed that very moment and asked Jesus to forgive me of my sins and save me for eternity with Him in heaven.

What about you? When did you tell God, "I believe! I believe that your Son, Jesus, paid the penalty I deserved for my sin. Please forgive me of my sin and make me clean"?

Still, I did not completely understand the heart of the Father. So I continued to pray that same prayer, asking God to save me, for the next five or six years.

Through discipleship I began to grow both in the knowledge of God's truth and in its application for my life. I was both surprised and thankful to learn that I could be certain of my salvation. God had me the first time I had prayed. After I finally became sure of "being saved," I grew through the next years at a spiritual warp speed.

My heart was a sponge and took in everything I could learn about Jesus. After a season of intense growth, I took all my newly obtained knowledge and, with great pleasure and a bit of arrogance, drew a different, bigger box around God. I decided

Daily Prayer Praise

The Counselor, the Holy Spirit, whom the Father will send in my name, will teach you all things and will remind you of everything I have said to you.

John 14:26

that everything that could be known about God was inside my box. It felt good to finally understand Him and own enough theology books to make me feel really smart about His character and His ways. Essentially, I thought I had God mostly figured out.

One of the walls around my new box had to do with the Holy Spirit. As far as I knew, the Holy Spirit came to live inside of you at salvation. He was God's presence and seal. He would intercede. He would comfort. He would convict and He would guide. I believed I would mature spiritually because the Holy Spirit would guide me into deeper knowledge and help me keep the walls of my spiritual box tight and secure. The Holy Spirit would keep out anything that did not fit neatly into my own personal systematic theology.

I knew of others who wanted the filling of the Holy Spirit, but for some reason I was satisfied with just the assurance of His presence. Being filled with the Holy Spirit was outside my information and tradition. Pursuing knowledge and personal discipline was more in keeping with my training and understanding.

Here's what I want you to get before I did: being completely filled with the Holy Spirit is desirable above all other spiritual pursuits. Ordering your life around the pursuit of the Holy Spirit is the right order. From His fullness in you, every desire of God for you is free to be released and followed.

Maybe you have drawn a box around God too. If you have decided that He only works in certain ways and not in ways unfamiliar to you, then you have a box. If you have rejected "fullness of the Holy Spirit" teaching in the past, I want to assure you that God is outside your box, waiting for you to peek around the walls of your knowledge and see Him as He is—working powerfully in the lives of believers through the fullness of His Holy Spirit.

> Ordering your life around the pursuit of the Holy Spirit is the right order. From His fullness in you, every desire of God for you is free to be released and followed.

List some of your ideas about the Holy Spirit. Or maybe you'd rather list your questions about Him.

Just as "God was pleased to have all his fullness dwell in [Jesus]" (Col. 1:19), He longs to have His fullness dwell in us. Later in Colossians, Paul wrote, "You have been given fullness in Christ, who is the head over every power and authority" (Col. 2:9).

What do you think *fullness* means here?

What kind of empty places do you have right now?

Do you believe the fullness of God could fill these places?
☐ yes ☐ no **Why or why not?**

As women in love with God, we have certain responsibilities that come with our relationships. Of primary importance is that you and I make our hearts available to God's desire to fill us with the Spirit. In this week, as much as I know how, I want to continue to direct you in this journey toward the fullness of the Spirit.

There is a difference in the woman who is saved and getting by as best she can and the woman who is saved and living every day of her life filled by the power of the Holy Spirit. The first woman is a carnal Christian, and the second is a spiritual woman. We could say that the second woman is dancing. The first one continues to walk according to her old desires, and the other is being led by the Spirit of God. There is only one degree of choosing that separates these women. But as it turns out, one degree makes all the difference.

Would you end today's study with your own heartfelt prayer? Tell God you want to be led by His Spirit.

Day 2

The Work of the Holy Spirit

We continue this week with a bit of a theology lesson, but I hope you really enjoy learning more about the power that is transferred to us at salvation through the third person of the Trinity, the Holy Spirit.

Daily Prayer Praise

But you will receive power when the Holy Spirit comes on you; and you will be my witnesses in Jerusalem, and in all Judea and Samaria, and to the ends of the earth.

Acts 1:8

When you are saved, several things happen:

> *The Holy Spirit has opened your heart to pay attention and receive the Word of God* (**Acts 16:14**).

> *God has called you and drawn you to believe in His Son, Jesus Christ* (**John 6:44; 1 Cor. 1:24**).

> *The Holy Spirit has crucified the old sinful self* (**Gal. 5:24**).

> *And the Holy Spirit takes away the power of sin* (**Rom. 6:6**).

Through repentance, the woman who is saved turns to Christ as her Savior and begins the process of setting aside the sins that have plagued her life. At the beginning of our life in Christ, we are spiritual babies.

Remember Paul's words to the Corinthians:

> *Brothers and sisters, in the past I could not talk to you as I talk to spiritual people. I had to talk to you as I would to people without the Spirit—babies in Christ. The teaching I gave you was like milk, not solid food, because you were not able to take solid food. And even now you are not ready. You are still not spiritual, because there is jealousy and quarreling among you, and this shows that you are not spiritual. You are acting like people of the world.*
> **1 Corinthians 3:1-3, NCV**

We begin as babies, and it's important for us to remember that God has great patience with new believers. He understands the weakness by which we begin. Just learning about grace. Only beginning to walk by faith and battle our old sin patterns. The very good news is that there is hope for those of us who struggle in earnest to become women of great faith. There is a place in Christ for the stragglers and beginners and stumblers.

Maybe you realize that God has had great patience with you over the years, starting and stopping, flourishing and fading.

There is a place in Christ for the stragglers and beginners and stumblers.

Take a minute to remember God's patience and thank Him for His kindness toward you.

We all come to Jesus as beginners and babies. And many times we can find ourselves back at the beginning again. Thankfully, none are ever turned away from the grace of God. All of us have a certain hope because of God's patient mercy and love.

Scripture says that even though we come to Christ as a spiritual baby, from our gratitude for God's magnificent grace to us, we are called to grow up in His mercy. To graduate from baby milk to solid food. This whole study we have talked about growing up in faith. This week, I want you to know that the power to grow is given to each of us through the indwelling of the Holy Spirit.

Becoming a mature spiritual woman requires the next step of choosing. That one degree of difference is the way of becoming a woman of righteous confidence. The woman who is becoming spiritual is being filled and refilled by the powerful presence of the Holy Spirit. The abundant, full life that Christ promises in John 10:10 comes to us from the full indwelling of the Holy Spirit in us.

Do you remember the disciples after Jesus had called them? Their next three years were spent with Him as God in the flesh, and yet Jesus lived outside their bodies. They walked with Him, ate with Him, and witnessed His miracles with their own eyes. But Jesus did not yet live inside of them. What we remember about the disciples during those days is their weakness, their lack of confidence, and their struggle with pride. Many times, they gave up on the Savior, denied Him, fell asleep on Him, and fought over who would be the greatest in His kingdom.

I came to give life—life in all its fullness.
—Jesus, John 10:10, NCV

But the night before His betrayal, Jesus promised the disciples that the Holy Spirit would come after Him to live inside of them and give them power. That same promise holds for every believer today.

> *"I will ask the Father, and he will give you another Helper to be with you forever—the Spirit of truth. The world cannot accept him, because it does not see him or know him. But you know him, because he lives with you and he will be in you."*
> **John 14:16-17,** NCV

Jesus' final words of instruction to the disciples just before He ascended into heaven was our prayer verse today:

> *"Wait here to receive the promise from the Father which I told you about … when the Holy Spirit comes to you, you will receive power."*
> **Acts 1:4,8,** NCV

On the Day of Pentecost the promised Helper called the Holy Spirit came to live inside of the disciples.

All of them were filled with the Holy Spirit.
Acts 2:4

Using the following Scripture references, note what the disciples were like before Pentecost and after Pentecost.

Matthew 8:25; 19:13; 26:40	
Mark 9:17-18,32-34	
Acts 4:8-13; 6:2-4	

After the promised indwelling of God was given to the believers, the rest of Scripture testifies to the radical difference this new power made in the hearts and lives of the disciples.

○ The light of Christ came into the darkness of their hearts. Where the light filled, darkness was removed. Though still completely human, this light of God inside them made them holy.

○ The timid and fearful disciples, once consumed with pride, became humble servants who were bold enough to speak even though threatened with death. Their works changed. They spoke with confidence. Their hearts broke with compassion for the lost and the suffering.

○ The Holy Spirit changed the disciples' relationships with one another. His indwelling love began uniting them as one body. They put off bickering and selfishness. They sold their possessions to care for one another and welcomed strangers they saw with new eyes. They understood their place in God's calling with a new heart of compassion and resolve.

I don't know about you, but too many times I have been a whimpering, fearful disciple, obviously not operating in the fullness of the Holy Spirit. More than anything, I want every facet of my life to be radically changed and impacted by the same anointing and indwelling the disciples received.

Day 3

How the Holy Spirit Works

With all my heart, I believe that God intended for regular women like you and me, with everyday concerns and everyday lives, to live powerful, confident lives because of the filling of the Holy Spirit. Maybe we have been wallflowers, but I believe God longs for us to dance.

Certainly, the most prominent question in this pursuit begins to be *How?* How do I give myself to the process of filling? What is my part in being filled by the Holy Spirit? Is filling something that continues to happen unconsciously after I become a believer, or do I have a role?

As we look to Scripture to answer the question of *how?* let's first consider the building blocks of truth about the Holy Spirit.

- ☐ The Holy Spirit comes to live inside the person who has accepted Jesus as Savior **(Acts 2:38-39).**
- ☐ The Holy Spirit exists to mediate our relationship with Jesus, to make Christ real to people, and bring glory to God **(John 16:14).**
- ☐ The Holy Spirit does what He pleases. He acts according to His will **(Heb. 2:4).**

We cannot manipulate the presence of the Holy Spirit. He comes to us at first as a gift and then more fully according to His own will. Jesus says the Holy Spirit is as free as the wind (John 3:8). He cannot be seen or controlled. He goes where He pleases. He is free.

So now what? If the Holy Spirit is free to go wherever He pleases and He only moves at His own will, then what do we possibly have to do with the pursuit of His presence in our lives? How does a woman seek the fullness of the Holy Spirit in her everyday heart and life? The testimony of the Holy Spirit in Scripture gives us more direction.

Acts 10 tell us that before Peter finished preaching, even before an invitation was given or the last hymn was sung, the Holy Spirit came.

Daily Prayer Praise

For you did not receive a spirit that makes you a slave again to fear, but you received the Spirit of sonship. And by him we cry, "Abba, Father." The Spirit himself testifies with our spirit that we are God's children.

Romans 8:15-16

> *While Peter was still saying this, the **Holy Spirit came down** on all those who were listening.*
> **Acts 10:44, NCV, emphasis mine**

We just learned that the Holy Spirit has a free will. Peter could not make Him "fall upon" those who were listening that day, but I believe some correlation exists between what Peter was preaching or how he was preaching and the coming of the Spirit.

From the passage concerning Peter's preaching in Acts, we read that Peter was preaching many truths about Jesus. Jesus as the Peacemaker. Jesus as Lord of All. Jesus anointed with the Holy Spirit and power. Jesus stronger than sin and Satan. Jesus who was raised from the dead. Jesus the final Judge of every person. And Jesus as the forgiveness of sins. Do you remember that one of the purposes of the Holy Spirit is to glorify God?

From this passage, it seems that the Holy Spirit is more likely to come where the truth of Jesus is clearly being spoken. Where Jesus is being lifted up. Where we have made Jesus and His character the focus of our attention. The Holy Spirit is appointed to glorify the Son of God, and I believe that He comes to give fullness to the life that has centered itself on Christ.

I am praying that you consider your life with the Lord. I am praying that you choose to intentionally step into the spiritual life of maturity and growth. God gives the help necessary for each of us to step over, grow, and become. He meets our need through this powerful gift of the Holy Spirit. If we are to know Him more fully and operate in His power, I believe our first priority is to take the story of Peter's teaching to heart and center our lives on Jesus.

I am a bit hesitant about the next thing I feel led to do. I want us to walk through the different areas of our lives to evaluate where we are and what needs to happen so that we live more Christ-centered. My hesitation is that you could misunderstand. Outlining these thoughts might begin to feel like a list of rules or things you have to be in order to manipulate the Holy Spirit. I'll say it again. All of Scripture testifies that the Spirit is free to work according to His will. We cannot make up rules to legislate His work. But our lives can make Him welcome and invite His sustained presence.

So we'll begin today with these areas and continue in tomorrow's study. Let's begin with these questions:

"If I am lifted up from the earth, I will draw all people toward me."
—Jesus, John 12:32, NCV

Areas of Your Life

Your Mind

As you consider your thinking life, what do you find? A woman who longs for the Word of God? His guidance? His principles? His direction? Or a woman who has forgotten about the power of the Word to give life? Have you become a woman who thinks apart from the Spirit?

> *Those who live following their sinful selves think only about things that their sinful selves want. But those who live following the Spirit are thinking about the things the Spirit wants them to do. If people's thinking is controlled by the sinful self, there is death. But if their thinking is controlled by the Spirit, there is life and peace.*
> **Romans 8:5–6, NCV**

I realize that we live in a world that dumps much unavoidable garbage into our minds. I also realize that you are a grown-up who should be able to filter out what is inappropriate for a godly woman to keep stored. But for the woman who is not intentionally removing the evil, the garbage can really stack up fast.

Consider what you watch, maybe not once but repeatedly, over and over, becoming desensitized to its content. What do you read? Study? Meditate on?

Who do you listen to? Who speaks the truths that shape your thinking? How do you feed your mind? Where do you turn for advice or counsel? How could you begin to exalt Jesus with your thinking?

We will turn to more areas of our lives tomorrow, but for today are we mentally welcoming the Holy Spirit to fill our minds with His presence? Explain your answer here.

Day 4

More Work of the Holy Spirit

Daily Prayer Praise

In the same way, the Spirit helps us in our weakness. We do not know what we ought to pray for, but the Spirit himself intercedes for us with groans that words cannot express.

Romans 8:26

Yesterday we talked about living as women who invite the work of the Holy Spirit. Let's pick up with the next area to consider:

Your Countenance

If I were the Holy Spirit, and we're all certainly glad that I'm not, I just wouldn't want to live inside some people. Grumpy people. Perpetually angry people. Vindictive people. A petulant, sulky countenance is not very inviting to anyone and probably not to the Holy Spirit as well.

I realize that we all have gloomy days and times of sadness, but if the countenance is a reflection of the heart, what would yours usually reveal? How about your general disposition? Do people regard you as negative? Angry? Pessimistic? Apathetic? Do you invite the Holy Spirit to come and abide powerfully in your life through your countenance? Or do you imagine He'd want to avoid you?

Look at what the Spirit can do with your temperament:

> *The Spirit produces the fruit of love, joy, peace, patience, kindness, goodness, faithfulness, gentleness, self-control.*
> **Galatians 5:22-23, NCV**

Would you make Him welcome in your life? Submit your countenance, humble your attitude, and lift up Jesus with your life so that He can produce the fruit that will transform your nature.

Your Home

You may think this is a bit over the edge, but I am fiercely protective of the things and people that come into my home. I am working really hard to create a haven of peace and respite for my family. I want this setting to be inviting to the Holy Spirit. I want my children to know what it feels like to live where the Spirit lives, and I want them to know the difference when they are apart from Him.

I have put copies of Scripture and references to the Word all through our home. I filter the television. None of the children have Internet privileges. No one can watch a movie at home or even away without permission. Where there is coarse talk, there are serious liquid soap consequences. Everyone knows I'll sit all their friends down and have a "Come to Jesus" meeting at the drop of a bad attitude. I want it to be fun here. I want them to dance here. I want Jesus to be exalted here.

> *The Lord is your protection;*
> *   you have made God Most High your place of safety.*
> *Nothing bad will happen to you;*
> *   no disaster will come to your home.*
> *He has put his angels in charge of you*
> *   to watch over you wherever you go.*
> **Psalm 91:9-11, NCV**

As you look around your home, what do you see? Invitations to walk in peace and holiness? Reminders of the love of God and His good gifts to you?

Do your surroundings invite the presence of the Holy Spirit or do they cultivate darkness and the presence of evil? I realize this may be misinterpreted as legalistic or small-minded, but I will not allow either the presence of evil or a representation of evil in our home. I'll do whatever is necessary to have it removed. We have enough to battle. Evil and its subtle incarnations are not welcome here.

> *Hate what is evil, and hold on to what is good.*
> **Romans 12:9, NCV**

Your Choices

Here's where I may really begin to get on your nerves, step on your toes, or both. I believe I am to speak boldly in these next ideas, but please hear my heart of grace in these thoughts.

As believers, we might read all the right things and think on the Word of God, seek Him in private prayer and in public worship. We can have a radiant countenance that perhaps just comes naturally. We may have a distinctly Christian home that valiantly proclaims our beliefs and rejects evil. We may even work in ministry or a Christian profession where all day, every day, is devoted to making Christ known. Many people live in just this way. And yet, many of these Christians are choosing poorly.

Do your surroundings invite the presence of the Holy Spirit or do they cultivate darkness and the presence of evil?

The Scripture is very clear in its call to live in obedience. Some things aren't even gray. The line is not blurry. No speculation is needed. I will be the very first in line to celebrate all the freedom that Christ has given to us. As a matter of fact, in most of my teaching I find myself working hard to set women free from the bondage they have known—all in the name of religious rules and misapplication of Scripture. But today I want to speak to obedience in your choosing. If we desire to live in a way that makes the Holy Spirit welcome, choices really matter. OK, buckle up.

> *If we desire to live in a way that makes the Holy Spirit welcome, choices really matter.*

☐ You cannot have sex outside of marriage. Obvious, I realize, but it's amazing how many Christians disregard this very clear teaching, especially older singles. Seems like the young kids have been zealous in their commitment to wait. Many of us need to decide that we will wait again. (See 1 Thess. 4:3-5.)

☐ You cannot get drunk. Again, duh, this one is not some obscure, irrelevant Bible teaching. It's meant for us, the believers who want to pursue the heart of God. In case you missed it, really great Christians make very stupid choices when they are drunk. (See Eph. 5:18.)

☐ You cannot watch evil or invest your time in evil. Include here all forms of pornography, pornographic magazines, romance novels with explicit sex that stimulate sexual urges, and chat rooms that conduct lewd conversations. It's sick to me that hotels report their highest levels of pornographic viewing when they are hosting a pastors conference. And women are not excluded from this category. What would the history page on your computer reveal? I realize you can be a lonely single or a lonely married woman, but you just cannot go here. Take up knitting. Go down to the homeless shelter and help somebody. Get help for yourself. Do whatever it takes to break such habits, because you cannot indulge your curiosity or the sickness any longer. (See Ps. 101:3.)

☐ You cannot cheat, steal, or covet. Again, this teaching is blatantly evident throughout Scripture, but Christians are cheating and wondering why they have no power in their lives. Work hard in the direction of your desires, but you cannot shortchange the process by cheating. Scoundrels will encounter consequences. (See Ex. 20:15.)

○ You cannot be lazy. Well you can, and some believers are, but you must realize sad repercussions follow your poor choices. (See Prov. 6:9-11.)

Clearly, Scripture issues a very specific call to obedience. Much of that obedience affects our personal and private choosing. But as much as Jesus offers His free grace and mercy to all of us, His call to obedience cannot be ignored.

Clearly, Scripture issues a very specific call to obedience.

Read Leviticus 26:3-43. Yes it's long and in Leviticus, but it has practical application.

What is your immediate reaction?

God's heart has not changed since the Old Testament. Being obedient to Him can change your life.

Obedience is living grateful for God's goodness. If you desire the presence of the Holy Spirit, I am very certain that He cannot come with fullness into a heart of willful disobedience.

Day 5

Led By the Holy Spirit

My girlfriend said to me the other day, "I had forgotten that the Holy Spirit is the third part of the Trinity, equal in importance to God the Father and God the Son, Jesus. He is God's presence on this earth in this age. He is God's hand to hold and God's voice to listen for."

How many of us feel the same way? We have forgotten about the weight and significance of the Holy Spirit. He is in and around us, and yet we miss the glory of His presence. But that is the work of Satan. His chief concern is that we do not see the glory of God. And very specifically, if you have not given much thought to the work and the magnitude of the Spirit in your life,

Daily Prayer Praise

God did not give us a spirit of timidity, but a spirit of power, of love and of self-discipline.

2 Timothy 1:7

then you are actively missing the glory. Paul tells us about these designs of Satan in 2 Corinthians 4:4 (NCV):

> *The devil who rules this world **has blinded the minds of those who do not believe.** They cannot see the light of the Good News—the Good News about the glory of Christ, who is exactly like God.* **(emphasis mine)**

One of the ongoing questions that we can ask ourselves is:

Am I seeing the glory of God?

When we can see the glory of God, then we want to honor the Christ of that glory. We want to see more of the Holy Spirit's efforts around us. We want to celebrate His goodness and worship His splendor.

How do you see God's glory around you today?

Another question is:

Am I being led by the Holy Spirit?

I find myself dealing with this question most often when I am disciplining the children or searching for a way to unlock their hearts or give guidance. Many times I will be talking to a woman at a conference and I have to wait to respond to her until I believe I am being led by God's indwelling. Sometimes after a woman has told me her circumstances, I'll realize that I don't have any idea what to say to her. Several times I have asked if I can e-mail her later or speak to her at another break. I don't want to give her anything until I believe I am being led by the Spirit.

What are the questions in your own life where you need to be led by the Spirit?

God has every answer that we need. He is always willing to lead in your decisions and your words. Romans 8:14 puts it this way:

The true children of God are those who let God's Spirit lead them **(NCV).**

And then Paul writes in Galatians:

Live freely, animated and motivated by God's Spirit **(5:16, MSG).**

We get our new life from the Spirit, so we should follow the Spirit **(5:25, NCV).**

You can know that you are being led by the Spirit because the following types of evidence will show up in your life:

- ☐ Your actions or choices will not run counter to any teaching from Scripture.

- ☐ The Holy Spirit makes your desire to please God stronger than your desire to operate according to your flesh or please only yourself.

- ☐ Being led by the Spirit brings freedom (2 Cor. 3:17) instead of feeling like you are forced to obey a law with one arm twisted behind your back. Obedience in the Spirit brings joy instead of a burden.

Obedience in the Spirit brings joy instead of a burden.

- ☐ The woman who is being led by the Spirit is a woman characterized by loving behavior (Gal. 5:13-14).

- ☐ Being led by the Spirit produces the fruit of the Spirit in your everyday, moment-by-moment life: love, joy, peace, patience, kindness, goodness, faithfulness, gentleness, and self-control (Gal. 5:22-23).

- ☐ The heart being led by the Spirit is thankful for every gift that God brings. A woman full of the Spirit is really grateful.

Every once in a while, one of the children will do the same old thing, like throw their dirty clothes behind the door in the bathroom. Then from somewhere I hadn't expected, I will hear myself respond to them in a fresh, new way. My discipline to them comes through words of patience and self-control, and I will know that I am being led by the Spirit.

How do you know when you are being led by the Spirit?

When I was a young believer, acting in obedience felt like a duty, but as I desire more to walk by the Spirit, obedience is producing a freedom and a joy that I did not know in those early years.

The next question that should work its way through our spiritual life is:

Am I praying in the Spirit?

The Bible directs us several times to pray in the Spirit. Praying in the Holy Spirit means that we are moved to pray and guided in prayer by the Spirit. In Ephesians 6:18 Paul says that all our prayer is to be offered in the Spirit; so praying in the Spirit isn't just some different form of praying, it's how God expects that we will learn to pray.

In Romans 8:26 Paul wrote about praying in the Spirit:

> Also, the Spirit helps us with our weakness. We do not know how to pray as we should. But the Spirit himself speaks to God for us, even begs God for us with deep feelings that words cannot explain **(NCV).**

So we know that the Holy Spirit helps us in our weakness, even our weak praying.

Praying in the Spirit enables us to pray in ways we could not on our own. Perhaps the question rising inside of you at this point is one that I have dealt with:

How do I know that I am praying in the Spirit?

As I realized that I could pray in my own strength or I could pray in the power of the Spirit, I truly desired the latter, but how? No one ever taught me to "pray in the Spirit." I have come to understand two very important elements that we can apply and then rest in.

First, to pray in the Spirit requires faith.

Second, to pray in the Spirit requires that we pray according to God's Word.

Right now, in my mind, I am choosing an area of my life where I completely want to be led by God's Holy Spirit. Choose yours. And let's pray together, in complete faith, according to the Word of God, to be led and directed by the power of the Holy Spirit.

A study of the Holy Spirit ought to get more than a week, but I am praying that this week of lesson is more than theology to you. I pray that by understanding the Holy Spirit more, you will see the glory of God and live inside His presence.

A Note From Angela

Dear friend,

I have thought about you and prayed for you every day as I prepared this study. I am praying today that these past weeks have been like fresh oil for your faith in Christ. I hope you have met with God in new and exciting ways, that your passion for God has been stirred, and that your soul longs to dance for His glory!

Today I am writing this note to you between Thanksgiving and Christmas, one of the busiest times of our year. I am filled with joy and just about bursting over the goodness of God. I love everything about these days, and I especially love having my family close and orchestrating the activities, scents, and sounds of what will become their tender memories of Christmas.

My deep contentment comes from the fullness of Jesus inside. I want to evidence a daily surrender and an ongoing desire to grow in every circumstance. I want to choose to love Him well and live out His promise to bless a surrendered life. This tender blend of my choosing plus God's promise becomes like a dance for His glory.

I have talked to two friends today who are not dancing. Neither one is facing tragic circumstances. Each one has been incredibly blessed with family, friends, and God's provision for every need.

They both belong to God. Each friend attends church, Bible studies, and small-group meetings with her spouse. Neither has any joy. I mean none. Empty. Sad. Mad.

We talked and prayed and looked at each other with tears. Both of my friends must surrender their hearts and choose maturity over selfishness. In many ways, they know what they must do. Each one waits for another way or a different answer or someone to make it all better. Don't get me wrong, I'm speaking not from superiority but from surrender. I have been these women at various times in my life. We all know it's a miserable place to be, especially since God has called us to so much more.

I am praying that here at the end of this study you are choosing to grow up in the ways of God. That your heart has remained on His altar and your soul is growing up in your faith. Oh my, what a life you will live if only you will stay in His presence and grow up in His truth.

I love you, my friend. God willing, one day we will meet face-to-face and you'll tell me, "I'm a dancing girl." We'll share a big hug and dance a little jig, and God will shine all around you.

More than anything ... love God with all of your heart, mind, soul, and dance! Dance the dance of your life for the glory of God!

Angela

Prayer

Father,

Thank You for sending the Holy Spirit to live inside of me. Thank You for loving so much and filling me with the power to live a righteous life.

Lord, use this week to teach me about Your Spirit. I want to understand and learn. I want to be filled to the measure of all fullness. All that You have promised is my desire. To walk according to the Spirit is my commitment. To listen for the guidance of Your Spirit is my intent. Teach me more. Lead me in the application of these truths.

And Lord, let me dance. For Your glory and forever in Your presence ... let me dance.

Amen.

Leader Guide

This leader guide will aid you in facilitating small-group sessions for *When Wallflowers Dance*. A leader kit is also available (item 005094538), which contains two DVDs with video messages for your seven-session study, one CD-ROM with materials for the retreat, and one DVD with selected video messages and special clips for the retreat format. While using the video sessions will enrich your study, you may choose to use only the member book.

If you are leading this study without using the video messages, the introductory session is optional. Having an introductory session gives you time to get acquainted and distribute member books; however, if you decide to forgo the introductory session, make sure participants receive their member books in time to complete the first week of study before session 1.

If you use the video messages, the introductory session will be a time for those interested in the study to come and preview the material. The member book is not needed for this session. Having an introductory time will allow you to see how many women are interested in the study and thus how many small-group leaders you will need. It provides a time to collect money for and distribute member books; see how many women will need childcare; decide on the best time and dates for everyone involved; and encourage women to invite their friends, neighbors, and colleagues to the study. Once you know the number of children, arrange for childcare during your session times.

When Wallflowers Dance is a study for both believers and those who have not yet made the decision to follow Christ as their Savior. The study focuses on questions and feelings all women share, no matter their age or life experiences. The study is an opportunity for women from your church to invite unchurched friends and neighbors to participate with them.

You can plan meetings for 60 to 90 minutes. The video teachings range from 18 to 42 minutes, so make sure you leave enough time to watch the video at the end of the session. Arrange to have a TV and DVD player in your room for each session.

If you will have more than seven or eight women in your study, you may want to consider having multiple smaller groups. Smaller groups encourage women to be more open about sharing. Recruit one leader for each small group to help facilitate discussion. You may have multiple groups at different times, or you may choose to have small groups that come together to watch the video at the end of the session.

Each small-group leader will need to complete each week's assignments and encourage the women in their group to do the same. The women will receive much more benefit from the study if they choose to participate fully in all six weeks.

As a leader, you do not have to know all the answers, but you should be familiar with the material and be willing to help answer questions. You can format each session around how much time you wish to have for discussion. Don't feel pressured to go over every question in the leader guide; the questions are a starting place for your group to discuss what was meaningful to them each week. Try to keep the women on topic while allowing them to transition into issues that affected them in the week's lessons.

The leader guide splits each session into the following:

Before the Dance
Indicates preparation needed for the session

Get En Pointe
An opening activity or discussion time

Getting to Know Your Partner
Discussion questions that break down the key points of each week

In His Arms
Prayer time

A Dancing Lesson
View the teaching video from Angela Thomas

Remember, these are just suggestions. Identify those areas where you were touched during the week, and bring those up for discussion in your group. Pray together, cry together, and definitely laugh together as you learn how to stop being a wallflower and get out there on the dance floor.

Introductory Session

Before the Dance

1. Read "About the Author" (p. 4) and the introduction (p. 5). Be prepared to share information about Angela Thomas and the study with your group.
2. Have copies of *When Wallflowers Dance* available to distribute.
3. Create a sign-up sheet with spaces for the name, address, phone number, and e-mail of each participant. Have pens and extra Bibles available.
4. If you wish, provide light refreshments each week. You may also decide to decorate the room in a way that incorporates the theme of the study—a big vase of flowers in the middle of the room would be a simple but beautiful touch, or you might use posters of different types of flowers.
5. Hang a long piece of paper on the wall to use as a banner. Provide markers with which to write on the banner (make sure they won't bleed through); you may also wish to bring flower-themed scrapbook supplies to spice up the visual effect.
6. Cue the introductory session, "Come to the Altar," on your DVD player.

Get En Pointe

1. As women come in, have them sign in on the prepared sheet. Show the women where to find the banner, markers, and other supplies. Ask one woman to write "GROW UP" in big letters in the middle of the banner. Ask another to write out 1 Peter 2:2-3 somewhere on the banner. Instruct each woman to write out one way she has tasted that the Lord is good. If time permits, they can also draw and decorate the banner. This banner should be hung up in the room for each session.
2. Share the information you prepared about Angela Thomas and the study of *When Wallflowers Dance*. Explain that each week is split into five daily sessions with questions to answer. As they study each week, women should highlight

and underline phrases and questions they want to talk about at the next session.

Getting to Know Your Partner

1. Explain that in the following sessions members will spend time in small groups discussing questions pertaining to their week's homework.
2. Ask the women to explain what they wrote on the poster.

In His Arms

1. Ask women to share prayer requests in pairs. Spend time in prayer for one another.
2. As the women finish, have one leader pray 1 Peter 2:2-3 over the group.

A Dancing Lesson

1. View "Come to the Altar" on DVD 1 [18:41].

After the session, collect money for member books and distribute the books to those who plan to participate in the study.

Session 1

Before the Dance

1. Complete all assignments in week 1 of the member book. Preview the session 1 video.
2. Place the sign-up sheet, extra member books, pens, and Bibles on a table at the entrance to your room. Decorate and provide refreshments if desired.
3. Have dry-erase board or posterboard and appropriate markers available.
4. Cue the DVD to session 1.

Get En Pointe

1. In your large group, ask: *Have you ever received any kind of inheritance?* If women are comfortable doing so, ask them to share what they received.
2. Share that in this week you discovered the treasures of your inheritance, and in this session your group will discuss them further.

Getting to Know Your Partner

1. What kind of altar did you make for the activity in day 1?
2. What feelings did you circle on page 8? How have they affected your mood lately?
3. Ask for volunteers to read aloud the following: 1 Chronicles 6:49; Psalm 141:2; Revelation 8:3. Did you realize the significance of the altar? How does it make you feel to be participating in such a long tradition, dating back to the Israelites in the wilderness?
4. Share answers to the questions on page 17 about living the "resurrection life."
5. Review the six numbered "Treasures of Our Inheritance" from days 4 and 5. Which most caught your attention? Which surprised you? Consider writing down the points on

a dry-erase board or posterboard and brainstorming under each one:

    —What were some the key points about this treasure?

    —What would you have to do to live this out in your life?

    —How does knowing this make you feel?

6. Read aloud the following verses about being a child of God: Isaiah 49:15; Matthew 7:11; 23:37; 2 Corinthians 6:18. How do these reassure you? What characteristics of a child's life did you note on page 22?

In His Arms

1. Pray Acts 20:32 over your group of women.

A Dancing Lesson

1. Watch "The Wallflower" on DVD 1 [41:24].

Session 2

Before the Dance

1. Complete all assignments in week 2 of the member book. Preview the session 2 video.
2. Place the sign-up sheet, extra member books, pens, and Bibles on a table at the entrance to the room. Decorate and provide refreshments if desired.
3. Cue the DVD to session 2.
4. Copy the following passage onto a dry-erase board or poster board: *Now, pile up decades of those things for all of us, and the soul grows weary. Dreams fade. We can become numb. And many of us try to stay numb. Trying not to feel because feeling might hurt again.*
5. Provide colored index cards for the prayer activity.

Get En Pointe

1. Welcome women back. Encourage them to keep doing their homework and coming to the session even if they haven't completed all the assignments.
2. Direct the women's attention to the place where you copied the passage from the member book. Ask: *What things lead to these kinds of feelings in a woman's life?* You may want to record their answers under the passage you wrote.
3. Explain that this week you studied the "un-woman," and today you are all going to talk about escaping from the "un-woman" life and becoming a woman of godly passion.

Getting to Know Your Partner

1. What was your understanding of an "un-woman"? Did you see characteristics of an "un-woman" in yourself?

2. How did you answer the question on page 29—"Why aren't we becoming the women we have always wanted to be?" Be as specific as you'd like.
3. Enlist women to read aloud Ephesians 4:14-16, preferably in several translations (it is written out in *The Message* paraphrase on p. 32). Share responses to the questions following the passage on pages 32-33.
4. What were some of the goals you listed (p. 33)? Brainstorm steps you all can take to help one another meet your goals.
5. What do you think about taking some time off from commitments to focus on your relationship with Jesus? Would it be possible for you? Your gut reaction might be screaming no, but take time to really think through it.

In His Arms

1. Instruct women to form groups of three or four. Give each group a stack of colored index cards. Ask each woman to write one or two prayer requests down, one per card. Then women should trade prayer-requests cards. Ask the women to pray throughout the week for the requests on the cards they have. If a Scripture comes to mind that could pertain to a specific request, they should write that passage on the back of the card. Ask them to bring all the cards back next week.
2. Ask the groups to pray briefly for each other's requests.

A Dancing Lesson

1. Watch "A Clean Life" on DVD 1 [40:46].

Session 3

Before the Dance

1. Complete all assignments in week 3 of the member book. Preview the session 3 video.
2. Place pens and extra Bibles on a table at the entrance to the room. Decorate and provide refreshments if desired.
3. Cue the DVD to session 3.
4. Print out "Paul and the Conscience" from the CD-ROM (Session 3 Handout), and make enough copies for all the women in your group. Use the handouts in question 1 of "Getting to Know Your Partner."
5. Bring a bag of inexpensive chocolates to share with the women.
6. Have a dry-erase board or posterboard and appropriate markers available.

Get En Pointe

1. Greet each woman as she enters, giving each a chocolate.
2. Once it is time to begin and all the women are settled, ask: *For how many of you is chocolate a guilty pleasure? Why or why not?*
3. Explain that today's session is about guilt and the conscience and will expand on Angela's ideas regarding a clean conscience.

Getting to Know Your Partner

1. Distribute the handouts you made in "Before the Dance." Take turns reading aloud the Scripture; then discuss the follow questions: What was Paul's idea of the conscience? How do we keep our conscience clear?
2. Do you think it's easier to "come clean" when you've lived in so-called despicable sin or in more casual, unintentional sin?

3. Do you relate to this passage from page 54? *Most of my life, guilt somehow seemed righteous. In my immaturity, I believed that if I kept flogging myself before God, He'd be happier with me because of my shame.*
4. Do you tend to fish for old sins, or are you able to accept God's forgiveness and move on? How does your reaction correspond with Micah 7:18-19?
5. How do you think the guilt process progresses from temptation to guilt? Consider using a dry-erase board or posterboard to sketch out what your group says about the temptation-to-guilt process.

In His Arms

1. Return to the same small prayer groups you formed in session 2.
2. Ask women to return the prayer-request cards to the original requestor. Ask them to share any changes in the situations for which they requested prayer, and spend some time together praying over each situation again.

A Dancing Lesson

1. Watch "Resisting Bitterness" on DVD 2 [29:46].

Session 4

Before the Dance

1. Complete all assignments in week 4 of the member book. Preview the session 4 video.
2. Place pens and extra Bibles on a table at the entrance to the room. Decorate and provide refreshments if desired.
3. Cue the DVD to session 4.

Get En Pointe

1. In your large group, ask: *What is the difference between pain and bitterness? How are they related?*
2. Tell the women that this week of study dealt with bitterness and the choice to cling to God's promises or relish bitterness. Remind the women of the benefit of doing all their homework and attending each weekly session.

Getting to Know Your Partner

1. Ask: *To what degree do you think people around you would describe you as bitter? If so, about what?*
2. Share your responses to this question from page 73: Which of God's promises do you need to recommit to believing today?
3. Read aloud Romans 3:10-24. How do we get rid of our bitterness?
4. Do you have a favorite verse in Proverbs? Why should we choose wisdom? Check out your list on pages 79-80. Would you share one thing you might change to be more wise?
5. What did you think about this quote from Oswald Sanders? *God does not waste suffering, nor does He discipline out of caprice. If He plow, it is because He purposes a crop.*

In His Arms

1. Ask each woman to spend two or three minutes in private prayer, conversing with God about any bitterness in her own life. End this time with a prayer thanking God for promising to bind up the brokenhearted and release the prisoners.

A Dancing Lesson

1. Watch "Not Yet" on DVD 2 [39:45].

Session 5

Before the Dance

1. Complete all assignments in week 5 of the member book. Preview the session 5 video.
2. Place pens and extra Bibles on a table at the entrance to your room. Decorate and provide refreshments if desired.
3. Cue the DVD to session 5.
4. Arrange for a friend to call you on your cell phone at the time your session begins.
5. Have a dry-erase board or posterboard and appropriate markers available.

Get En Pointe

1. Greet women as they come in. Begin to praise them for sticking with the study—only one week left!
2. Around this time, your phone should ring. Go out in a hallway and stay there for two or three minutes. When you return, ask: *Did it bother you to wait for me? Are you patient in your waiting, or do you sigh when people have 11 items in the 10 items or less line?*
3. Explain that today's session is about waiting on God.

Getting to Know Your Partner

1. Which of the "waiting" passages on page 88 did you star? Which spoke most to your situation of waiting?
2. Consider the elements of effective waiting outlined this week. Which speaks to you most? Jot them down on a dry-erase board or posterboard, and then brainstorm about why we need to do these, what the key points were for each, and how we can implement them in our lives.
3. Is there a Christian woman you really admire who has mentored you in your journey? Is there someone you might consider asking to be a mentor for you?

4. Share answers to this question on page 101: In what areas of your life have you already done everything and realize that God is asking you to stand and wait?
5. How can you help other women in this group to stand? How can they help you stand?

In His Arms

1. Stand together and pray, asking that God will give you strength to stand when the Enemy wants to beat you down. Ask God for guidance and tools to help your wait.

A Dancing Lesson

1. Watch "The Holy Spirit" on DVD 2 [32:00].

Next week is the last session. Because the video is much shorter than in previous weeks, you may wish to have some sort of celebration. Before the women leave from this session, decide if you want to have a small party after session 6; if so, arrange for women to bring food, decorations, music, and so forth.

Session 6

Before the Dance

1. Complete all assignments in week 6 of the member book. Preview the session 6 video.
2. Place pens and extra Bibles on a table at the entrance to your room. Decorate and provide refreshments if desired.
3. Cue the DVD to session 6. Also, have DVD 1 ready to play the "When Wallflowers Dance" music video.
4. Ask two or three women to prepare to share the stories of their salvation.

Get En Pointe

1. Have the pre-appointed women share their salvation stories. Make sure to say that if anyone has questions or wants to talk about salvation through Christ, they can speak to you after the session.
2. Congratulate the women for making it through the study. Explain that today in your small groups you will discuss the power of the Holy Spirit.

Getting to Know Your Partner

1. As members are comfortable, share answers to the questions pertaining to the fullness of the Holy Spirit on page 107.
2. What were some of your ideas of the Holy Spirit when you were a child, teenager, and even before this study? Did your perception change this week?
3. Read aloud 1 Corinthians 3:1-3. What is the difference in talking to a new believer and a more mature believer?
4. What changes in the disciples did you note on page 110? What does this say about the power of the Holy Spirit?

5. What has been the most poignant life lesson for you during your study of *When Wallflowers Dance?* Do you think it will change how you live? How?

In His Arms

1. Watch the "When Wallflowers Dance" music video on DVD 1. Ask women to pray silently while they reflect on the study.
2. Hold hands and have a popcorn prayer. You needn't go around the circle; just appoint one person to start and one person to close. Ask the women to pray for one another, that they will implement any lessons learned in the study, and also for any other prayer requests they have.

A Dancing Lesson

1. Watch "Eyes to See" on DVD 2 [20:15].

If you planned a celebration time, enjoy! Discuss the idea of doing another study with this same group. You can explore *www.lifeway.com* for other great studies from LifeWay Church Resources, or see the handout "Additional Resources" on the *When Wallflowers Dance* CD-ROM.

Retreat Guide

Welcome to the Retreat Guide for *When Wallflowers Dance!* This guide will outline ideas for a Friday and Saturday retreat; however, you will want to do what works for the group you are in. Please take this time to read Angela's "Letter to Women's Ministry Leaders" on the *When Wallflowers Dance* CD-ROM. It will give you more ideas for where, when, and how to lead a retreat of this kind.

You will want to assemble a steering committee of people to help put together the event. Involve as many women as you can in the preparation phase. If women feel a sense of ownership, they will bring more guests and make the entire experience more effective. Enlist leaders for the steering committee who will in turn enlist others for their teams. Adjust the number and size of teams to fit your church size. In some situations more than one church may want to work together to have a women's retreat. Women will need to be in charge of the following things:

1. The **Administration team** will conduct sign-ups and collect money; make arrangements with the place you will stay; arrange for a large TV or projector and DVD player; provide copies of quiet time guides and small-group leader materials (available on CD-ROM).

2. The **Publicity team** will spread the word about the retreat around your church and community. Postcards and posters are supplied in the *When Wallflowers Dance* leader kit, and a promotional video clip is available on the Retreat DVD to use as you wish.

3. The **Hospitality team** will arrange the Friday night dinner, Saturday breakfast, Saturday lunch, snacks, and drinks; put together a group to prepare, set up, and clean up if needed.

4. The **Creativity team** will gather materials for name tags, banner project, and any fun early bird/night owl activities your group plans; set up and clean up materials for these projects.

5. The **Worship team** will plan two short worship services with times of music, prayer, Scripture, and sharing.

6. The **Small-Group Leaders:** You will need one small-group leader for every five to seven women who come on the retreat. These women will lead three guided small-group sessions during your retreat time; questions for them to ask and consider are provided for you on the *When Wallflowers Dance* CD-ROM, along with a handout with Scriptures for Small-Group Time 1.

Retreat Schedule

Friday Night

5-6 p.m.	Registration, make name tags
6:00 p.m.	Welcome dinner
7:00 p.m.	Watch Retreat Clip "Welcome" [01:50]
7:10 p.m.	Retreat leader announces schedule for week-end and any other information needed.
7:15 p.m.	Opening Worship Time
7:40 p.m.	Watch "Come to the Altar" [18:41]
8:00 p.m.	Banner Project
8:30 p.m.	Small-Group Time 1
8:55 p.m.	Watch Retreat Clip "Good Night, Sleep Tight" (1:48)
9:00 p.m.	Dismiss to Quiet Time 1
10:00 p.m.	Bedtime/night owl activity

Saturday

6:00 a.m.	Early-bird activity
7:00 a.m.	Breakfast
8:30 a.m.	Watch "A Clean Life" [40:57] and Retreat Clip "Quiet Time" [03:07]
9:15 a.m.	Dismiss to Quiet Time 2 and break
10:30 a.m.	Watch "Resisting Bitterness" [29:47]
11:00 a.m.	Small Group Time 2
11:45 a.m.	Lunch
1:00 p.m.	Quiet Time 3
2:00 p.m.	Watch "Eyes to See" [20:15]
2:25 p.m.	Small-Group Time 3
3:00 p.m.	Closing Worship Time and Sharing
3:30 p.m.	Watch Retreat Clip "Good-bye" [01:48] and dismiss

Early-Bird and Night-Owl Activities

The women on your retreat have set aside time to get to know God and one another. Facilitate some fun for them! Bring board games and movies; have some sort of silly competition; paint finger and toenails and do each other's make-up; or just spend time hanging out in your PJs and talking. There are more ideas in Angela's "Letter to Women Ministry Leaders" on the CD-ROM.

Name Tags

Consider one of these ideas for name tags—

1. Use cut-outs of flower shapes.
2. Press dried flower stickers onto sticker or reusable name tags
3. Prepare tags in a variety of pastel wildflower colors.
4. Write names across packages of flower seeds decorated with raffia bows.

You may want to use the name tags to split your group into small groups of five to seven women for the breakout sessions. For example, all the "daffodils" are in one small groups, all the "roses" in another, and so forth.

Banner Project

Hang a long piece of paper on a wall to use as a banner (make sure the markers won't bleed through). Provide markers with which to write on the banner; you may also wish to bring flower-themed scrapbook supplies to spice up the visual effect. Ask one woman to write "GROW UP" in big letters in the middle of the banner. Ask another to write out 1 Peter 2:2-3 somewhere on the banner. Instruct each woman to write out one or two ways she has tasted that the Lord is good. If time permits, they can also decorate the banner. Let this banner stay hanging for your entire retreat.

Note to Leaders

You may choose to have this retreat to kick off a seven-session study of *When Wallflowers Dance*. Please note, however, that the video sessions on the retreat are the introductory session and sessions 2, 3, and 6 in the seven week study. Some of the quiet-time material is repeated in the daily homework in the member book. While the member book contains much additional material, women participating in the retreat and study should be aware that there will be some repetition. You may choose to skip the introductory session if you have already had a retreat introducing the material. You may also decide not to reshow the videos they have seen on the retreat.